THE MIND
THAT CHANGES
EVERYTHING

Dr Ian Gawler OAM
BVSc, MCounsHS

PLEASE NOTE

The information and suggestions in this book pertaining to imagery and meditation are presented only as material of general interest and not as a prescription for any specific person or any condition in a specific case. The reader is advised and encouraged to seek the aid of a qualified health practitioner for advice pertaining to his or her particular conditions and needs.

Published by Brolga Publishing Pty Ltd
PO Box 12544 A'Beckett St Melbourne Australia 8006
ABN 46 063 962 443
email: sales@brolgapublishing.com.au
web: www.brolgapublishing.com.au

The right of Ian Gawler to be identified as the Author of the Work has been asserted by him in accordance with the *Copyright Amendments (Moral Rights) Act 2000 (Cth)*

Copyright 2011 © Ian Gawler

National Library of Australia Cataloguing-in-Publication entry

Gawler, Ian, 1950–
The mind that changes everything : 48 creative meditations that will enrich your life.
9781921596995 (pbk.)
Meditation.
Mind and body.
158.12

Printed in Indonesia
Cover design by David Khan
Typeset by Imogen Stubbs

IAN GAWLER

THE
MIND
THAT CHANGES
EVERYTHING

48 Creative Meditations that will Enrich your Life

'Imagination is more important than knowledge.'

Albert Einstein

CONTENTS

CHAPTER 1

IT IS ALL IN THE MIND –
At least that is where it starts

I MAGINE THIS.
As a young decathlon athlete and veterinarian, I
developed a particularly difficult cancer that I was fortunate to overcome using techniques of the mind. Since
then I have worked for over thirty years with people who
were intent on their wellbeing and developing their mind
power to enhance their health, their capacity to heal.
Also, I have been fortunate to study for many years with
those extraordinary masters of the mind, the Tibetans.

While in recent years great minds of the Western
World have gone into physical laboratories to study
the truth of the physical world (and more recently the
mind itself), for hundreds, even thousands of years, the
great minds of the East went into inner laboratories to
study the truth of their minds. My main teacher, Sogyal
Rinpoche, the renowned author of *The Tibetan Book of
Living & Dying* has a remarkable capacity for translating

this ancient wisdom – the technology of the mind – into a modern context. So I have been fortunate to be able to combine access to learning from such an authentic and knowledgeable source with the opportunity to work with thousands of people doing their best to use this active form of mind training.

What is the most important thing I have learnt?

Whatever you do begins with a thought. Reading this book seemed like a good idea at the time. Whatever you are sitting on to read this book began in someone's mind as a thought: I will build a chair that looks and functions according to the image I have of it in my mind. Whatever it is that you will do when you put this book down will be determined by your mind. What you will have for your next meal begins with a thought. The next person you spend time with, the next outing with friends and family, the next business decision, the next holiday, purchase; on and on.

Everything begins with the mind.

However, there is more to it than this. While everything we do begins in the mind, what we complete, what we achieve, what we let go of, what we abandon; all these outcomes are largely a function of our own mind.

Truly, it is the mind that changes everything.

What then do we know of this mind?

For many it would seem remarkably little, even when we include the scientists of our day who study and attempt to heal it. Dan Siegel is a world authority on neurobiology and the mind. Discussing the mind with him recently, he informed me that of over 90,000 mental health professional he has asked in gatherings all around the world, well over 95% admitted that in all their training, whether as psychiatrists, counsellors, psychologists, nurses, etc., they had not one lecture specifically on the mind. They studied it for years, yet no-one even defined it.

So what is it? What is the mind?

Take a moment, do your own mental check and attempt to define what your mind is. If you find this challenging, at least you are in good company. The world literature on the mind is famous for either avoiding defining the term, or at least being remarkably vague about it. Many neuroscientists simply say they do not know what the mind is, while large numbers of philosophers say that even attempting to define it is futile, unhelpful and that it is a mistake to try!

In 1992, Dan Siegel began a four and a half year discussion group with 40 scientists from a wide range of disciplines. Their aim? To define the mind. Nearly twenty years later, Dan still regards his definition as a work in progress. But with all the people he has had interactions with over the years, no-one has improved on this one, while many are startled by it at first!

> **DEFINITION: The mind is an embodied and relational process that regulates the flow of energy and information.**

To fully understand this definition you may find it helpful if we attempt to explain the terms a little first, and then contemplate the words as a whole.

Let us start with the meaning of "regulates the flow of energy and information". Of course "regulates" means to control; but what is being controlled? "The flow of energy and information." The mind regulates how we use energy; what comes in and what goes out. In crude terms, it decides what we eat and drink, what exercise and activities we pursue. It regulates how we use our energy. The mind also has the capacity to gather, to store and to control the way we use information. It decides what we read, what we learn, even how we learn, and then it uses that information as it sees fit.

The mind has the potential to change everything.

What then of "the mind is an embodied and relational process"? Embodied first: the mind exists in a manner that is intimately connected to our physical body. While it is concentrated in the brain, it is widely accepted that the mind is not confined to the brain. In fact it even extends beyond the nervous system generally and is to be found actively functional in all parts of the body. Yet you can pull the body apart and you will not find "the mind". "The mind" is to do with the body, but it is far more than a part of the body.

Next we need to be aware of one of the most important qualities of the mind. You can change it. We used to laugh at the old, somewhat sexist maxim, "it is a woman's perogative to change her mind". Good news! We all can do it. In fact, the exciting new field of neurobiology that focuses on neuroplasticity clearly establishes that the brain and mind are far more flexible and malleable than we ever thought.

It is not so long ago neurobiologists taught that the brain actively developed up until the age of around five to eight years. This theory dictated that all was set in proverbial concrete around that age and the brain only deteriorated as we became older.

The concepts, knowledge and clinical experiments connected with Neuroplasticity have changed all that. Neuroplasticity refers to the brain's ability to change its structure and function according to how we use it. Norman Doidge's groundbreaking book *The Brain that Changes Itself* has eloquently described the advances in the current understanding that likens the brain more to our muscles than our bones. Even our bones do change a little over time but our muscles respond rapidly to whether we use them or not. Importantly, when we choose to, we can train our muscles – and they respond.

Neuroplasticity tells us the thrust of this particular book is sound. As with our muscles, we can learn how our mind works, train it and have it function more effectively. When we train our mind, we can rely upon it to bring us better health, more effective healing and profound happiness.

Before we launch into the techniques, let us return to the definition. The mind is "a relational process"; it exists within the context of relationships. All that we do depends upon our relationships – those we have with our environment, other living things and ourselves. Because we have a relationship with our self, we look after it. Depending on the quality of that relationship, we look after our body better or worse. Not many people self harm by actually cutting their bodies; some do, but many self harm by eating badly or not exercising. Many trash the environment and treat other creatures or people badly because they have a poor relationship with them. So the mind is a process that is affected by relationships.

That leaves "process" to consider.

Process is defined in the *Oxford Dictionary* as "a continuous and regular action or succession of actions occurring or performed in a definite manner". Take a moment to consider this, and be prepared to become a little excited. The mind being defined as a "process" means that it is an active "doing", not a sedentary object.

When all this is put together, these words define the mind not as a passive noun but as an active verb!

Viewed this way, the mind is well described as an emergent property. This means it is fluid, active, constantly changing. The mind exists in close relationship to our body, but is not our body, not even just the brain. The mind functions in relationship to all around us. It is affected by the environment we are in, the animals and the people we interact with. The mind regulates all our vital functions. It collects, stores, retrieves and uses information. It controls the energy that flows through us: physical, emotional, mental and spiritual.

It would have seemed totally remiss to write a book on the mind and to claim it changes everything and not to define what is the mind. For many such a definition is elusive, yet I am of the view that Dan Siegel's is excellent. It is well worth taking the time to sit quietly and contemplate its meaning. We will discuss contemplation later as one of our very useful mind training techniques, but in essence it is simple. Sit quietly, learn the definition, close your eyes and reflect on its meaning. Whenever your mind wanders onto other things or spaces out, notice you are off track as soon as you can, be gentle with yourself and simply return to your contemplation. Practising active reflection like this takes a thought from being nebulous and fleeting to something you anchor firmly in your understanding.

When you do this, you will have even more clarity regarding why we say "It is all in the mind". It is the mind that regulates and changes everything.

But how does it do it?

Everyone knows the neurobiologists say we use only a fraction of our mind's potential. What this book will help you with is how to use a little more of that potential.

There has been a conscious choice with the book to focus on the techniques that tap into those extra potentials of the mind and to leave for others to write about the scientific truths related to the wonders of the brain and the theories behind all this.

However, what we are talking of here is definitely a science. A mind science. This is how you train your mind. It is just like choosing to become physically fitter; going to the gym, running around the park, training your muscles. Here, however, we go to the 'mental gym'. Train our mind, enjoy it becoming fitter, more capable; get the best out of our mind and its potential.

Before the techniques, one more important consideration. The mind can be classified in various ways. One obvious classification is to talk of the conscious and the unconscious and we will discuss how we use both at length. However, there is a more profound classification vital to be aware of and this classification informs the contents of the book.

The mind has two aspects. It has the 'thinking mind' and the 'nature of mind'. The thinking mind is the aspect we are most familiar with and it is this aspect that contains the conscious and the unconscious minds. It is the thinking mind that has to do with everyday functioning. It is changing all the time as thoughts come and go. It is this aspect of the mind we train and can use for great benefit.

The nature of mind is a term used to describe that more profound aspect of our mind that is stable and enduring. This aspect of our mind is capable of being aware of our thoughts and is at the core of our being. It is constant; a source of inner strength and confidence, and it is the aspect of mind we come to experience in the deeper stillness or silence of meditation. This aspect will be referred to a little in this particular work but there is far more detail in the book I co-authored with Paul Bedson *Meditation – an In-depth Guide* which expounds on the nature of mind and how to experience it more directly.

What we are interested in here is how to use our active mind more fully. How can we be free of negative or destructive states of mind? How do we develop the clarity of mind to make good decisions and use our mind constructively? How do we train our minds?

The secret lies in understanding the primary way in which the mind functions. The key to this understanding is that we think in images, fantasise in images and plan and remember by using images. We also live in a world of images. Images are thrust at us via the media and advertising. It seems clear that successful people use imagery naturally and effectively. We all do to some extent, but most have little training in how to use this key to the active part of mind. This book then is offered as a user's guide to the inner workings of your mind – the use of imagery.

Imagery is a wonderful inner technique that has transformed many lives. Its dramatic benefits are to be seen in sport, business, relationships, healing, and in personal development and spiritual practice.

What then has been learnt from three decades of studying this field and helping others to apply the techniques in all aspects of their lives? What I have become to know is that imagery is dynamic, powerful and fun; it is challenging and transformative. However, it also has the capacity to be a double-edged sword. While overwhelmingly my experiences with imagery have been positive, it is also a technique that can be destructive.

Therefore, with this book I have aimed to detail the wide range of imagery-based, mind training techniques that I have used regularly and can share from direct experience. These techniques range across the breadth and depth of life. In fact, much of my work has involved participating in the intensity of people's lives; often after they have been confronted by life-threatening illness. The gravity of these situations has cut through any waftiness or impracticality and led to the heart of the matter – what to do, what works, how to deal with any complications. This aspect of my work has been a great testing ground for the development of these techniques.

In a way, it has been a delight at other times of my life to be able to go beyond the challenges of illness and to work with so many well people. People who are interested in performing at their best; in fulfilling their potential. So a lot more has been learnt from working closely with sporting and business people, those seeking more peace in their lives, and those who are really yearning for a direct and profound spiritual experience.

The point is, the techniques in the book are based in life. They are based on real life experiences and are well tested. Imagery certainly does have its pitfalls, so it is necessary to allude to these clearly throughout the text and provide clear direction on how to avoid them. However, the emphasis will be on what does work and how you can proceed into your own direct experience of the wonderfully creative realm of imagery.

The book itself represents a major re-write of my previous work *The Creative Power of Imagery* first published in 1997. While largely re-written and updated, many of the stories and techniques included here were included in that first book. The methodology is well tried and tested.

This is dynamic work so I am happy to receive correspondence on your experiences. Also, The Gawler Foundation is the organisation I helped to establish and a place that can assist if you find questions or difficulties arise and you need personal assistance. This said, the best safety net to offset any problems with imagery is to practise meditation on a regular basis. This will provide a balance and a calm grounding for the more dynamic inner work of imagery.

CHAPTER 2

THE MIND AND ITS BOUNDARIES –
Exploring limitations and possibilities

T HE MIND HAS an incredible capacity to both limit us and to set us free. The mind has the capacity to enable us to do what at first might have seemed impossible.

When I was eleven, I fell in love with high jumping. It was introduced to me by a rather fierce sports master; predictable in his fierceness, uncompromising in demanding the best of his students, and exquisitely subtle in giving praise indifferently. In short, this teacher scared the hell out of me, recognised a talent I had and demanded I discipline myself to develop it. After the first few terror-filled lessons, where I struggled to understand what was being taught, I soon felt the thrill of flying through the air effectively. High jumping became a passion. I jumped at school, my father built me uprights and landing bags and I jumped at home. It became a delight, an exuberant expression of youthful joy and vigour.

Then an extraordinary event occurred. When I was twelve, I was selected to represent my school at the Inter-School Athletics Carnival. The memory of the day stays clear in my mind. A large flat oval spreading out into just as flat parklands with only the occasional tree. Grass somewhat dried by the warm summer; a few greener patches from watering. A small crowd of parents and other competitors gathered around as the bar was steadily raised. A clear blue sky, as clear as could be. Radiant in my memory. The feeling of relief, hope and thrill as each of the other boys missed a height and dropped out of the competition. Then only me left, the existing record jumped and the bar continuing to rise. The feeling was new, magical. Nothing like this had happened before. It seemed so easy, almost effortless. The memory is of almost being in a dream at the time of each jump. On I go, the bar rising higher and higher until eventually I jump two inches over my head. Then it hits me. I look at the bar, now three inches above my head and suddenly it looks really high. I begin to think '*this is too high for me*'; I run in half-heartedly and do not look like clearing it.

Then the extraordinary. The local paper covers the competition and runs a small headline

'*Schoolboy jumps 2" over his head.*'

My passion for high jumping extends to athletics in general, and as I grow older I get into the habit of training regularly and experimenting with all the athletic events. It turns out I am reasonable at most, but not exceptional at any. So I become a natural for the decathlon, which combines 10 athletic events over two days. This collective event becomes a major focus of my life.

But here is the extraordinary bit. In my late teens and early twenties, I was fortunate to train under an exceptional coach, along with top athletes, including Olympians. High jumping remained my favourite event, although actually I did perform better at some of the other events. It came to puzzle me that, despite all the training, the coaching, the weight lifting, the experience, the enthusiasm, the wonderful peers; despite all of this, I never jumped higher than 6'4" (these were before the metric days). In fact I became quite reliable. I jumped that height, my maximum, at almost every important competition. Why never higher?

What a puzzle.

It was not until after I developed cancer, had my right leg amputated and learnt something of the mind and how it sets patterns in our behaviour that I made the connection: *Schoolboy jumps 2" over his head!* I had grown 6'2" tall. I nearly always jumped 6'4" – *2" over my head!*

Reflecting back to school days, each year I had jumped a little bit higher – as I grew! But how high? Probably you can guess – just 2" over my height; never more, never less! It seems I had formed an image of myself being able to jump that 2" over my head and it stayed with me throughout my athletic career. Anything more always looked too high for me!

So that informative experience I had as a 12-year-old, that experience full of emotion and energy, set in my mind a pattern which was at once both useful (jumping 2" over your head is not bad!), but quite restricting – I never jumped more than this.

Here is the contrast. Many years later I was approached by Debbie Flintoff-King for help in her preparation for the 400m hurdles before the Seoul Olympics in 1988. Debbie was hoping to learn how to relax and to sleep better before competitions. Also, she was concerned that imagery, or 'Inner Rehearsal', seemed to escape her. Ranked number two in the world at that time, she was worried she was missing out on a part of the inner game that might make all the difference for her.

Knowing I had been a 400m hurdler as well as a decathlete, and that now I had a deep interest in the workings of the mind and the techniques of meditation, relaxation and imagery, Debbie approached me for help. She had been given the impression imagery was important (true!) and that it required using a specific technique common to all, which is not true. Imagery has to be done in a way that works for the particular individual who is using it.

Debbie had been told by two well-meaning sports psychologists that to improve her performance by using her mind, she needed to create a mental image as if she was actually in her body and running a race. However, Debbie was unable to do this. All she could manage was to see herself running and hurdling as if she was watching herself on a video clip, but even then only vaguely. As we discussed her needs it became apparent Debbie felt there must have been something wrong with her. She blamed herself, rather than the technique she had been recommended.

As we talked more and watched footage of her races, it became obvious the first half of her 400m race was so strong, and she was so confident of it that it needed no attention. Whatever Debbie was doing there, it was working exceptionally well. Where there was a problem was that it was almost as if she went to sleep (relatively) on the second bend, getting little real drive as she almost cruised around the corner, before switching on again and coming home very powerfully. Debbie had an amazing finish.

So, we realised she needed a trigger to focus her efforts on the second bend. What she needed was to actually switch ON at the start of the second bend. She also needed to improve her hurdling style around the bend so she could alternate her leading leg going into the hurdles.

We began to work on developing imagery Debbie would find effective. This was achieved more through the use of words and feelings, rather than pictures. Debbie learnt to work in her mind on her hurdling technique by talking it through, by feeling the surge of power, by feeling coming home strongly and then feeling the delight of the end result – being up on the dais as she was presented with the gold medal. She learnt to rehearse her ideal outcome – in her mind and in her own way!

In reality, the race final was one of the epic races that make up Olympic history. As usual, Debbie ran hard, smooth and fast for the first two hundred metres. Then she switched on around the bend and drove on as she alternated her leading leg and hurdled strongly. Yet coming into the home straight she was placed only fourth and looked to most observers to be in a hopeless position. What few people realised of that race is Debbie ran her fastest ever time for her first 300 metres but despite this, there were still three women in front of her at that point.

Yet Debbie knew the power of her finish; she had an image of herself finishing hard and fast and she had a strong image of her victory. She never wavered. She never gave in; in fact, she just pushed harder. With each hurdle she drew closer. Over the last, it was just the Russian athlete Tatiana Ledovskaia who was in front. As the finishing line drew closer, the Russian appeared to slow – you could see the strain and relief on her face. She thought she had won and eased off a little. Debbie pushed on tenaciously. A lunge at the line and who had won? The Russian was announced first by the commentators, then indecision, then the replay and the official announcement. Debbie had won by the smallest of margins – one hundredth of a second!

Clearly, many things contributed to that memorable win – the hours and hours of unrelenting training, her husband Phil's amazing support and coaching, the sad death of her sister in an asthma attack just days before the race, Debbie's new-found ability to relax, and her motivation to dedicate her race to her sister's memory. Then of course there was her own intense desire to win. But also that inner image of winning, that belief created within herself and held to so clearly: the expectation of winning that had been built and reinforced by all that practice using inner rehearsal. Debbie acknowledges this inner work played a major part in what kept her in it when, despite her best ever first 300 metres, she found herself coming into the straight so far behind in the race of her life. She believed it was possible to win, she had a clear image of winning, and she pushed on to do just that in her own personal best and Olympic record time!

Thus, in athletics I personally experienced the limitations imposed by inner images, and yet I shared in the thrill of experiencing them working positively.

The truth is we live in a world of images. Images flood the world around us, being projected by television, film, photography and life itself. Everything we experience, everything that registers with our senses, forms an image that is taken in to be stored in our memory. Internally we think using images, remember using images, create using images. Our whole life is affected dramatically by the images that come to us or that we produce ourselves. Images have a major impact on what we accomplish as well as our health, our capacity to heal and our wellbeing.

As part of the inner work I did to overcome my own cancer more than twenty years ago, I used an active form of creative imagery. With my veterinary background, I was aware there are cells called osteoblasts whose job it is to remodel bone. For example, if you were to fracture a bone, your body would first form a large callus around the break, then lay down new bone on this framework. For a while, the repaired bone would appear on X-ray to have a solid lump of bone wrapped around the old fracture site. However, with more time, the osteoblasts would steadily nibble away the excess bone, remodelling the area so eventually it would look just as before – totally healed, even a little stronger now at the place where the break had occurred.

My cancer was an osteogenic sarcoma, which meant wherever it spread it grew new bone. So I began to imagine cells which I labelled as osteoblasts, nibbling away at this new and unwanted bone – a bit like bone-eating

'Pacmen'! Often I would reinforce this image and focus my mind even more by using a finger or two to touch the area I was concentrating upon. I feel sure this use of imagery was another helpful step in my recovery.

When in 1981 I began to help other people affected by cancer with a lifestyle-based self-help program, the core mind practice was meditation based upon relaxation and stillness. However, the more active, creative imagery work was taken up by about three quarters of participants and there were some remarkable results.

For example, Ellie was a young girl who was battling with an almost overwhelming brain cancer. When we first met, her mother had been told that Ellie was not responding to treatment, nothing more could be done for her and she only had weeks to live. On request, Ellie completed a series of drawings with me that proved to be both insightful and therapeutic.

When Ellie drew her bedroom, it seemed to me to contain an image that powerfully represented her cancer. Amongst her bedroom furniture she drew her dressing table with a large mirror above it. Here Ellie placed the only discordant image in her drawing – she scribbled heavily, angrily, wildly all over the mirror. When it came to depicting the outside of her house, Ellie had drawn a happy garden and a clothesline. So we put these images together and created a healing sequence.

Ellie was instructed to close her eyes, to relax a little and then to imagine the house and the clothesline. In her mind she then created what in one sense was a fantasy; however, the instruction was to imagine she actually was in this fantasy. Ellie began by moving to the back of the house. There she collected a bucket, filled it with water and took a cleaning rag off the clothesline. Next she walked into the house, up into her bedroom (which she had drawn on the first floor) and proceeded to wash off the mirror. The cloth became quite dirty, and she rinsed it in the bucket until the mirror was clean. Then she returned outside, flushed the dirty water down the gully trap, rinsed the cloth and hung it on the line.

Now Ellie had begun this in early December of the year we first met. At that time she was blind in one eye and her mother had been told by the specialists there was little hope of her living to Christmas. Early in the New Year not only was Ellie feeling much better but her sight was back to normal!

Then late in January a new development. Ellie's mother rang me, very disturbed, saying that having been in the routine of diligently practising her imagery morning and evening every day, suddenly Ellie had stopped, saying she did not want to do it any more. It seemed to her unnecessary and a waste of time. Ellie's mother was quite anxious, but I told her that often as people's physical condition changed, their imagery also could change. As recommended she returned to her doctors and thorough tests found all the cancer had disappeared! Ellie had made a remarkable recovery! Was she just lucky? Was the timing of starting the imagery just a coincidence? Maybe. But none of us closely associated with her at the time thought so.

On the other hand, I well remember a middle-aged woman, June, who around that same time was faced with advanced secondary breast cancer. June had been holding her situation stable for eighteen months. In many ways this was a remarkable achievement; yet she grew impatient, a little frustrated. Her husband Ken told me he accompanied June to a remarkable meeting with her cancer specialist. June was intent on finding out her prognosis. She wanted to know; in fact she had become obsessed with wanting to know how long the doctor thought she would live. Ken said the doctor was very reluctant to commit himself. He pointed out how well June was doing, and how he had not expected her to live as long as she had, but obviously something she was doing was working very well and she should keep it up. However, June was not going to be put off and kept on demanding a prognosis. Ken said that in the end, almost in frustration, the doctor offered what seemed to be a throwaway line, "Well, I guess three months would be a reasonable bet.'

June died three months later to the day! Ken remains convinced June fulfilled the image her specialist had so reluctantly planted there. It was, he said, as if she had suffered from the 'pointing of the bone', that ritualistic Aboriginal punishment that reliably leads to death with no physical cause or illness involved.

These examples serve to highlight that imagery has the potential of a double-edged sword. While clearly it is very powerful, imagery can have constructive or destructive effects, and when we come to use these images by conscious choice, we need to be confident we are using them in the correct way. So there is a real caution in the use of imagery and an imperative for you to feel confident when you use imagery in a premeditated way that the images you use are accurate, complete and that the practice is conducted in a positive state of mind.

For this is definitely a field of inner work where there is a right and a wrong way. Over many years now I have worked with thousands of people from all walks of life who have used imagery. Together we have learnt through experience, through mistakes, through successes. What I have observed is there are several major areas where imagery can have dramatic benefits. Also, what I have found is that many of the instructions available for learning imagery appear incomplete. Often books on this subject shout the positive possibilities which are wonderful, but they neglect to mention the very real pitfalls, or to give instruction on how to deal with the problems that regularly arise.

It is easy to find basic information, yet many people who begin to practise imagery tell me they have had unexpected experiences that the books or CDs do not cover and, which at the very least can be quite disconcerting, or at worst downright scary. Often the beginner can become confused or even disenchanted as doubts along with unexpected and sometimes disturbing images mingle with what they had expected to be a simple and powerfully positive experience

On top of all this is the fact that if you were to listen to some imagery exercises and were able to follow through and achieve what their suggestions allude to, you would end up in perfect health, with the perfect partner and job, incredibly wealthy and happy, and probably fully enlightened as well – overnight of course!

So what is real? What is possible? What is fantasy?

One of the main intentions of this book is to range over the very wide experiences that are possible; to indicate what is normal and reasonable; and to attend to what is unusual and problematical. The emphasis will be on problem solving and the effective use of these exciting techniques, exciting because the positive benefits are very real.

While for good reason I have started by sounding genuinely cautious, I do have direct experience of imagery playing a significant roles in improving performance in a wide range of human activities; effectively and positively changing deep-seated, destructive behaviours into constructive ones; powerfully fulfilling creative goals; enabling people to more than fulfill their potentials across a wide range of fields, including sport, business and relationships; enhancing wellbeing; being a catalyst in profound healing; and deepening spirituality in a transformative and sustainable way.

This then is intended to be a practical book. It is based upon my own range of life experiences, which include a history of competing seriously in athletics, a professional life as a veterinarian, surviving supposedly terminal cancer, assisting over 15,000 people directly with an innovative cancer self-help program and working with thousands more in workshops around the world. I have also worked directly with healthy top flight athletes and business people.

Unashamedly then, this book is based primarily on direct experience. While I have read widely on the subject, studied it, attended other people's workshops, and learnt directly from some remarkable teachers, my main teachers for this subject have been my own life experience and the many people who have worked cooperatively on imagery with me.

The theories we will expound to explain the nature of imagery, how it affects us and why it works, are to me common sense explanations of a basic human function. Most of us use imagery all the time, and do so with very little training, or even, in truth, little understanding.

What I hope to do in this book is to crystallise what I have learnt and offer it in the spirit of helpful sharing.

Now, a final proviso.

Everything you read in this book may be incorrect!

Incorrect! Why would I say that, you might well ask? Well, in this field particularly, you need to know that while imagery (and affirmations) are powerful, it is still quite possible to simply learn the techniques and to use them with little understanding. However, I believe that as these techniques depend upon using the creative power of your own mind, you need to own them. You are wise to take time to consider them, to reflect, to contemplate and to understand. For two reasons. Firstly, it is best if you take responsibility for your own actions and achievements! Secondly, because the more you understand and believe in what you are doing, the more effective it will be.

I will attempt to give you the best of what I know on all this. I invite you to discriminate. Experiment. Use what feels good and what resonates with your own integrity. Use what works and happily let go of anything else. Use these techniques not because I tell you to, but because you have considered them, understand their merits and are prepared to commit yourself. Hopefully, as you read, you will find what is presented here logical, sensible and practical; the sort of thing anyone can benefit from.

For that is the essence of the book—the lessons learnt by both ordinary and remarkable people who have used the creative power of their minds to good effect.

CHAPTER 3

YOUR INNER WORLD –
Exercises, definitions, theory and fun!

L ET US BEGIN with some simple, yet instructive exer-cises that help us to understand how images are used by our mind.

The Big Dog exercise

Wherever you are right now take a few moments to imagine a big dog. It may well help to close your eyes. Then allow an image to form in your mind of a big dog and take a few moments to notice what presents itself.

When you open your eyes again the first thing is to notice what feeling went with the image. Was it a warm and happy feeling, or was it an uneasy, even fearful one? In most groups, it seems the feeling response to the simple image of a large dog is about fifty – fifty. Half seem to like it and feel good about big dogs, the others feel unpleasant, maybe even becoming a little anxious just imagining a big dog.

So we learn straight away images are often very personal and that they will often have different meanings, different effects and different memories for different individuals.

However, there are some images, a select group of images, which can be described better as being 'archetypal'. Archetypal means a primordial or fundamental image that is interpreted in the same way by most people. In other words, an archetypal image such as water will have a similar metaphorical meaning to a middle European, to an Australian Aboriginal or a Chinese person. In virtually all cultures, water is a symbol of cleaning, of purity, healing, the water of life, a vehicle of spirit.

The point of this is that when you use imagery, unless you use archetypal symbols, you are best advised to develop and use images and symbols that are personally relevant and accurate. It would make little sense to develop any sort of metaphorical healing imagery using a big dog when such a beast scares you! This is why it is well worthwhile to have some knowledge and preparation before you begin imagery practice.

Back to the image of the big dog – we can learn more from it. What sort of big dog was it? A Great Dane? A Rottweiler? A German Shepherd? What were its features? What was it doing? In what context did you imagine it? Was it like a dog in space – was it just the dog you imagined with no background – or was your dog in a particular setting, like in a house, a garden, or a street? What were the details of your particular image?

It can be quite fun to ask some members of your family or friends to do this same exercise and to find out what they came up with. The diversity, the different range of images is bound to both amaze and fascinate you.

Now importantly, here is another key. There is no right or wrong in this. One person's image cannot claim to be better or worse than another's. However, it can rightfully claim to be different. So, again, very quickly we can notice the differences in both the details and the feelings that go with particular images, for particular people.

Take another moment now for this next, short exercise. This one is best done with your eyes closed and only takes about a minute.

Noticing your thoughts

Wherever you happened to be as you read this short introduction, simply close your eyes and notice what you are thinking about. Notice whatever thoughts are coming into your mind at this particular time.

You may have read another of my books, *Meditation – Pure & Simple*, where we use this exercise as a starting point to lead into the stillness of deep meditation. For some people, the remarkable thing that happens when they do this simple exercise is that their thoughts clear and they experience a few moments of inner stillness and peace – very directly and effectively. If you found you were one of those people whose thoughts did clear into stillness doing this short exercise at least you now have a great way to still your mind – simply observe your thoughts as an impartial observer and there you are! What could be simpler? It is worth pointing out that for some, meditation can be just that simple; for others this provides a starting point that the exercises in *Meditation – Pure & Simple* help to develop. However, that is not what the aim is here! We do actually want to come up with some thoughts so we can find out how we notice them!

Can I suggest, whether thoughts were noticeable for you or not when you did this short exercise just now, you take a moment for another short exercise.

Examining your thoughts

This time think of what you might do tomorrow. Again, it is probably best to close your eyes and then simply think about what you will do tomorrow. However, as these thoughts come to mind, aim to notice how it is that you are registering the thoughts; how is it that you are aware you are thinking?

What did you notice? As you were thinking of what you might do tomorrow, were you aware of the thoughts because you were noticing pictures in your mind, almost like watching video clips running through your head? Or was it more as if you were talking yourself through it, as if there was a conversation going on in your head? Or was it more like you were feeling your thoughts; as if you actually were doing the things you are considering for tomorrow? Perhaps you had one or two or even all three running at once?

It is probably worth taking a few more moments, just to check.

Re-examining your thoughts

So again, when you are ready, close your eyes and think about what you might do tomorrow. As these thoughts come to mind, notice how it is that you register them. Do you see them as pictures, hear them as words, or feel them like physical sensations?

What you learn from these simple exercises is which element of imagery is naturally predominant for you. Which one was it? Which did you notice most – pictures, words or feelings? Again, it is interesting to compare with others and notice the individual differences.

Another important thing to notice is the fact that our thoughts do come into our awareness as images. And not only thoughts.

An exercise in memory

Take a few moments to recall the building you lived in ten years ago. Probably best to close your eyes again and then recall where you were living ten years ago.

So how did you recall it? Did you see pictures of it? Did you see it from the outside? If so did you include the garden or the street? Or was it just the building you saw as if it was surrounded by black space? Did you see the inside? If so which room or rooms did you see? Did you travel through it? Did you see yourself in the picture or was it as if you were looking at your building in the way you look at things normally – as if through your own eyes?

But maybe you did not see the building so clearly. Maybe for you, you recalled your building by talking about it. If so what were the words? Were you talking to yourself: 'Where was I now; oh yes, ten years ago, I must have been nineteen, etc. etc.

Or perhaps you recalled it in still another way, a more kinaesthetic, feeling way and felt yourself in the home or felt the atmosphere of the home itself?

And what emotions came with the image? Did you feel happy, sad, neutral? Notice what an effect a simple image like your home of ten years ago can have on the way you feel.

What this last exercise does is to demonstrate the role imagery plays in the function of our memories. Memories are retrieved as images. Just as we become aware of our thoughts through the perception of images, so too we become aware of our memories via images.

In fact, there is more. This exercise demonstrates that the part of the mind where memory dwells, the unconscious realm of the mind, has its own language – the language of images. This is another crucial observation because the unconscious realm of the mind plays such an important role in our everyday life. As well as our memories, the unconscious holds our conditioning, our habits, and our beliefs. Throughout the book we will explore the pivotal relevance all this has in regard to our behaviour, happiness and health.

For now it is enough to recognise this significant principle and to observe that often we do not have direct or conscious communication with our unconscious mind. While it can exert powerful affects for good or bad, be constructive or destructive in our lives and also hold a huge reservoir of wisdom, for many people the gap between their conscious and unconscious minds is like that between two computers that speak different languages – like the IBMs and the Apple Macs of old!

What this all means is that if we choose to draw on the huge potential of our unconscious mind, to use it effectively and wisely, we need an interface. So this is another key principle of mind power – in imagery we have the common language that brings with it the potential to connect the conscious mind to the unconscious. Because the unconscious mind always functions using imagery and the conscious mind can learn quite easily to use or interpret images, we have the common language. This is a fact we will put to good use in several of the powerful applications of imagery discussed throughout the book where we will learn how to develop images with the capacity to positively influence our habits, conditioning and beliefs.

However, before we move on to the practical uses of imagery, and having already defined the mind, it is well to clarify what we are referring to when we use the terms Imagery, Visualisation and Affirmation.

The Oxford dictionary defines imagery as ' mental images collectively,' which really does not tell us a great deal! An image is defined as an 'artificial imitation of the external form of an object, a mental representation, a simile or metaphor or the character of a thing or person as perceived by the public'.

To image is defined as meaning to 'form mental images or concept of, to picture oneself (something non-existent or not present to the senses), to think or conceive.'

Given all that, here is the working definition for the word *imagery* as it will be used in this book

> **DEFINITION: Imagery is the conscious development and repetition of mental images and associated feelings for a creative purpose.**

Be reminded that images are composed predominantly of pictures, words and feelings. While the sense of taste and smell can add to imagery, usually they are not as significant as the three major senses of sight (pictures), sound (words) and touch (sensations).

Visualisation and affirmation are sub classifications of imagery. While imagery involves the use of any or all of the senses (and most commonly just three), visualisation in the way we will use the term here only involves the use of inner pictures, while affirmation is the use of the power of words for their own often remarkable effects.

So to be clear, imagery for some people may be practised primarily using only the pictures or the words or the feelings. While most people do use all three some of the time, most are predominant in one. What this means is that when it comes to how we think, particularly before we have trained our mind, we all tend to predominate in the use of one of pictures, words or feelings.

However, when it comes to developing the capacity of our minds and using imagery constructively, the more of the five senses that are developed and can be used together in an imagery exercise, the more potent that exercise becomes. We will return to how to expand our imagery in the most complete and effective way with the different exercises still to come. But clearly, visualisation uses only pictures, affirmation only words, imagery – all the senses possible!

The next exercise, however, will demonstrate another of the natural ways in which we use imagery every day. Imagine that for your next holiday you will have the time and money to go on the best trip you could ever hope for!

An exercise in planning

Take a few moments now to indulge this fantasy. Close your eyes, consider your choices, and plan your next trip, your next holiday. Where will you go? Who will you go with? How will you get there? What will you do once you are there?

What did you decide? Where did you choose to go? How did you get there? What did you do and, importantly too, how did all this feel? Did you feel a sense of delight with this simple fantasy? Did you feel a sense of frustration or disappointment, doubting the possibility or practicality of such a holiday trip? Are you about to run out and make the bookings? Again, notice the impact created by the suggestion to ponder a particular thought. Notice too that it is imagery you use for the thinking, for the planning.

As you consider the choices, in this case the range of holiday possibilities, it is imagery that is used to review the possibilities. Once you make your choice and plan how to get there, again it is imagery that is the key to the process of how you do it.

So, planning too is put into effect using imagery. What type of images predominated for you in this particular exercise? Pictures, words or feelings? Did any taste or smell come into it? Want to check?

Noticing the images of planning

Take a few more moments to fantasise over
the trip you might take for your next holiday. Notice how you consider the choices,
fix on one particular trip and plan how you
could do it. It will all be done with images.
Just check out now how you do it and what
type of imagery you are using.

This exercise in planning begins to reveal the very nature
of the mind itself. Basically, when you reflect upon it, it
is very evident that the most basic function of our mind
is to help us to survive.

The fact we humans are so dominant on this planet
certainly is not due to us being physically the strongest or
fastest. No, our dominant feature is the mind. Each of us
has a mind which has the capacity to register experiences,
record them, learn from them and then apply what we
have learnt in new situations – all with the intention of
doing whatever will give us the best chance of surviving,
and the best chance of being most happy. It is through
the use of our mind and its capacity to plan that we shape
our lives.

Perhaps the easiest way to understand how the mind
works in this way is to consider the holiday trip again.
Do the following exercise as a simple fantasy; just so you
can notice your mind at work.

An exercise in goal setting

Consider again where you might really go for a future holiday. There are probably many destinations you could choose from. Reflect a little and make a choice.

As you do this, you reveal one of the fundamental principles of how the mind works. While you begin by considering a range of possibilities, eventually you do choose one destination. You make a goal. Then with a specific goal in mind, planning becomes possible, it flows on naturally and the result you hope for (of actually getting there) also becomes a possibility.

This exercise demonstrates to us that the mind is goal-oriented. What we mean by this is that the mind likes to have a clear goal because once it has that clear goal it can begin to make the decisions and the choices that will most likely lead to that goal being fulfilled.

We can well describe the mind by saying it is a goal orientated, decision-making tool. A tool that ideally we use in the most effective way possible!

With the trip, once a goal is chosen, once you have selected your destination, it is time to decide on all the details: Will you drive, go by train, fly? What will it cost? Have you enough money already or how will you get it? When do you need to book? What will you take? On and on the planning goes as you do whatever it takes to fill in all the necessary steps to get from where you are now to where you want to be—fulfilling this goal.

These simple observations on how the mind works reveal two of the three major principles of what many people call "positive thinking"; setting a goal and following through. However, altogether there are three of these principles.

The three principles of positive thinking

1. Develop a clear goal.
2. Do whatever it takes to achieve that goal.
3. Choose to enjoy doing it!

The third principle—enjoy doing it—is also of major importance as it relates to our feelings. If it does not feel good, it is not likely we will persist for long, whereas if we are enjoying it and we are doing whatever it takes, we are almost assured of success. But realize the operative word is 'Choose'- as in "choose to enjoy doing it". Recognise the power of choice, for while in most situations if you have a clear goal, and are committed to it and are doing whatever it takes, you are almost certain to enjoy it, there may be other situations where it is tough going, there are hurdles to overcome or where a lot of perseverance is required.

Remember you have your own power of choice. When you recognise the truth of this capacity to choose, and then learn how to train your mind a little, you can choose to be happy, to be sad, to be depressed or joyful.

Now, if you are currently stuck in a particular emotion, especially if it is a strong one, this may see a little farfetched. You may feel initially, as many do, that circumstances dictate how you 'should' feel.

"Of course I am angry. Don't you know what he did to me?"

"Of course I am depressed. Just consider my life!"

However, be assured you do have this great freedom, perhaps the only true freedom, the freedom to decide how you will respond to your circumstances—the freedom to decide how you will feel.

Now this is not an invitation to suppress feelings, to feel guilty or shameful. But it is an invitation not to get stuck with these feelings. So, faced with any type of difficult situation you may well feel sad, angry or depressed. That could be both natural and reasonable. It is probably important, perhaps even essential, to acknowledge and express the full extent of any difficulties you may have, as well as sharing the feelings that go with them, before you are really free to decide more actively how you will respond to the situation. Once you acknowledge and express your feelings, you will have more freedom, more capacity to determine to do whatever it takes to fulfil your new goal and to choose to enjoy doing it!

I well remember my old friend George who provides a classic and very real example of all this. George was diagnosed with prostate cancer many years ago. George had left his home country and travelled half-way around the world to start a new life at the age of nineteen. He worked hard, married, raised a family and eventually developed a successful business. When George's cancer was diagnosed he was devastated. It was very advanced, widely spread throughout his bones and his doctors only gave him months to live.

George stopped work, locked himself in his house,

and with the blinds closed, spent most of the day crying. He did not talk to his wife or children when they came home in the evening. He put all his energy into suppressing his feelings, fears and tears, while he attempted to put on a brave, exterior front. Inside, however, he felt like a man just waiting to die.

Time passed painfully slowly. Then one day he went out for the paper and his eyes fell on my first book *You Can Conquer Cancer*. His eyes lit up with the title, he bought it, read it, and although he was very fragile, he thought perhaps it was worth a try. Inspired by the book and encouraged by his wife, George came to our groups and felt the hope rise within him. For the first time, he began to talk about his situation with his wife, then his children. They shared something of their own grief and fear. They did something new. They cried together. But then, with a new sense of possibility, they resolved to do something about it. George now had a new goal. He believed it was possible to get well again- he could imagine himself not only surviving, but enjoying life again.

George did many things, worked hard with great commitment and excellent support. He went on to have a remarkable recovery.

Two more exercises clarify another key point regarding how the mind works. Both these experiments take only a minute.

The White Horse exercise

Close your eyes again and this time spend a minute not thinking of a white horse. That is right, a minute NOT thinking of a white horse!

How did you go? For most people, that white horse just keeps on charging into their thoughts. It seems that trying not to think of it, just draws attention to it and makes it more of a focus.

The Red Rose exercise

This time spend a minute thinking of a red rose. Pay close attention to the details – do you imagine a rose in space, is it in a vase or on the bush? Is it an emergent bud or is it in full bloom? Perhaps you can even imagine its perfume or feel the stem and the petals. Just take a minute now to concentrate on a red rose.

Probably this latter one is the easier task to comply with. Focusing on a red rose for a minute is usually easy enough. This second exercise also holds the key to the white horse. The most immediate way to NOT think about something is to think of something else.

Most importantly, we need to be aware that attempting to NOT think of something actually focuses the goal-orientated mind onto that very thing – just as effectively as if you had chosen to think of it directly.

You can observe this principle at work when parents tell their children 'Don't walk in the puddles!' This draws the kids' attention to the puddles and in they go. And then the parents have the cheek to get upset after they have quite effectively, if somewhat unknowingly, directed them straight in!

How then do you tell a child to keep out of the puddles? Think of it for a moment. The mind is a goal-orientated, decision-making tool. You want the child to stay away from the puddles. You want the mind to focus away from the puddles. Where do you want the child to go? On the dry ground. So you say 'Keep on the dry ground.' Rather than telling them what not to do, you instruct them what to do.

Have you ever seen a child carrying a full bowl of soup? What is the natural reaction? To shout 'Don't spill the soup!' But what is it the mind registers? 'Spill' and 'soup.' So when the soup is spilled, there is just as likely to be another insult added to injury. 'You clumsy kid, why didn't you do what I told you?' The poor child not only feels guilty for making a mess but gets a negative affirmation as well. If the child was really aware, he would reply to the parent, 'But I did, I did what you told my mind to do!'

So how do you tell someone not to spill the soup? Think again—what do you want them to do?

Try 'Keep the bowl level.' It works just about every time.

These examples are fun yet quite illuminating. Most

children are barraged with negative affirmations as they grow up and are focused inappropriately in this way.

Likewise in adult conversations or at work, most of us have been taught to use the 'Don't do this or don't do that' style. So it can be very useful to listen to yourself and then make the effort to retrain yourself to use positive affirmations or directions. This can be done, but for most of us it takes a good deal of practice; so be gentle as you start to retrain yourself and persevere.

This same principle can be extremely important in healing. Many people facing life-threatening illness begin by being scared of dying. This is not surprising and often this fear leads to a high motivation to get well. However, if, as is often the case, the preoccupation is 'I don't want to die,' from the mind's point of view, what is the target, what is the focus? Obviously the dying! So, what is an important step in getting well? How do we aim for recovery? By moving the focus of our attention away from dying and onto living! What does the person want to live for? What is their reason for living? What is their passion?

This is obvious in George's graphic case. While he was feeling hopeless and full of fear of dying, he was hoping not to die but literally all he was doing was waiting around for it to happen. Once he became inspired and felt there was some hope for recovery, he was able to rekindle his natural love of life and set about living again. George's focus shifted from death to life and almost immediately healing began to flow.

This story makes it clear that in comparison with trying not to die, there is far more healing in focusing on living and living well. As we study all this, we soon come to realise we are healed by what we turn towards, far more than what we turn away from. When we affirm life, healing is a much greater possibility. Healing graphically demonstrates the importance of what we focus upon; another feature of the mind that is of great significance in every aspect of life.

Here then is a summary of what we have learnt so far about the mind and its potential

- The mind's creative power is vast, while its effects can be destructive or constructive depending upon how it is used.
- All the workings of the mind involve the use of images.
- Imagery is the conscious development and repetition of mental images and associated feelings for a creative purpose.
- Through imagery we can dramatically increase the creative power of our mind.
- Images can be personal or archetypal. Personal images will have different effects on different individuals. Archetypal images have a more universal impact.
- Our inner images are made up mostly of words, pictures and sensations. The other senses may be relevant, but commonly are less involved.
- Feelings are an integral part, in fact a crucial part of the effective use of imagery.
- Thoughts come to our awareness via images.
- Memories are recalled using images.

- Planning is carried out using images.
- Communication between the conscious and unconscious aspects of the mind is possible using the common language of imagery.
- The mind is a goal-orientated, decision-making tool.
- There are three principles of positive thinking:
    1. Develop a clear goal.
    2. Do whatever it takes to achieve that goal.
    3. Choose to enjoy doing it!
- The mind, as a goal-orientated tool, targets whatever is in strongest focus. Importantly, this focus can be expressed as a positive or negative – the red rose or the white horse.
- What we focus upon, significantly affects outcome. If our focus is on something that we may fear or are attempting to suppress, we give power to that very thing. Alternatively, when our focus is on what we are aiming to achieve, we give power to our goal.
- What we turn our focus towards has for more importance than what we are attempting to turn away from. Focus on the positive, the creative side of life!

Now that we have some understanding of the way our mind works, and the basic principles behind imagery, let us move on to consider how we can prepare to use creative imagery techniques consciously and effectively.

CHAPTER 4

SETTING CLEAR GOALS –
The wisdom behind imagery

T HE NEED FOR having a clear goal is probably fairly obvious. The real question is how do you set a clear goal? How do you decide what goals are really in your best interests? That is the deepest and most challenging question. Get this answer right and everything else is relatively easy.

So, given you have decided to go on a holiday, it may be easy enough to decide which destination you will go to. But what if you were to pause long enough to consider what else you could do with the time and money if you did not go on holiday at all. Then the possibilities open up endlessly. You could save the money, stay home and sleep. You could give some of the money away to a worthwhile cause or go on a retreat. You could borrow more money, stay home and spend the time extending the house. You could… you could…

How then do you decide? Are you a creature of habit

who goes on holidays because it is Christmas and that is what you always do? Do you rationalise the balance of work, play, rest and holidays and make a calculated choice? Do you go because the children demand it? Is someone else making your choice for you? Are you making your decisions for yourself? And if you are making your own choices, on what basis are they being made?

These are the sort of irritating and slightly provocative questions most of us prefer to defer. We probably put off the thinking and go simply because it feels like a good idea at the time! No real harm done with a holiday. But what if we use the same, rather casual approach for 'Which job will I take?', 'Where would I prefer to live?', 'What lifestyle will I adopt?'

Clearly, the big question is how to decide what goals to pursue? Perhaps it is worth taking a few moments to review the whole decision making process.

The first thing is to notice who it has been in the past that set your goals. Was it you, or someone else? Often this question is helped by actually contemplating the questions: who is living my life? Who tells me what to do directly? Or subtly? Who am I attempting to please? Or hurt? Who influences the decisions I make? Who affects how I live my life?

The contemplation on 'Who is living my life?'

Sit quietly as you might if you were in the practice of meditating. Close your eyes, relax a little and begin to ask yourself the question 'Who is living my life?'

Consider the influence any of the following may have: parents, children, partners, teachers, employers, employees, neighbours, media figures; the list can go on and on.

As you reflect on all these possibilities, you might think 'Wow, actually other people are doing it for me quite a lot.' If so, contemplate each of those people one at a time. Imagine them doing the things they do for or to you, reflecting on how it is each particular person is dictating terms in your life, making decisions for you, living your life.

Keep repeating the question to yourself 'Who is living my life?' and looking deeply into the answers, the people who come in response to the question.

Perhaps it is almost as if these people who are living your life make up a committee that collectively is in charge of your life. Between them, the committee tell you when you are OK, when what you are doing or thinking is OK, when you got it wrong, when you need to suffer! What a lot of power these people can have!

Contemplate "Who is living my life?"

Now, if, as many people do, you discover you have quite a committee living your life for you, you will probably realise they are something of a mixed bag! There will be the useful committee members, the teachers, the role models, the mentors. Probably worth keeping them. Then there will be those who are simply attempting to impose their will, their interests, their prejudices, their habits and desires onto you.

Probably worth being free of that lot!

When you are ready, try this great imagery exercise,

The exercise for unloading your committee

Imagine all the unconstructive, unhelpful people on your particular committee. Gather them together in your mind, then put them on an imaginary bus and take them for a long drive. Put them off the bus! Whoopee! Put a sign up on the front of the bus. No passengers! Leave the committee behind. Start driving your own bus!

There is another way you can do this contemplative exercise which you may find both helpful, fun and therapeutic. You will need blank A4 paper, a pencil and a rubber.

The exercise for reclaiming your life

Take a sheet of A4 paper and turn it on its side. Using a pencil, make a small egg shape in the middle and write 'ME' in it. Now draw pencil lines radiating like spokes to other eggs circling your own. In these outer eggs write the names of the people who live your life for you. Parents, children, partner, boss, employees, bank manager, lady over the back fence, etc. You may need a few layers of 'eggs' to fit them all in!

When you have completed the task, take a rubber and determine to make a change. Erase the connecting ties and as you do so, let each person go inwardly, as well as in this more ritualistic, visual way. Feel the release, the start of a whole new phase of your life.

Now, if you have decided to make your own decisions and set your own goals, how can you be confident you are on the right track? Do you just 'go with the flow' and allow circumstances around you to decide? Do you attempt to reason it all out and be very logical? Do you hope for revealing insight and the assurance of wisdom? How do you know you are doing the right thing?

In practical reality, you probably use a bit of everything, however, when it comes to the crunch, the guts rule! Many decisions are dependent upon other people, many are made on the run in response to immediate pressures, influences and opportunities. Reason is useful and wisdom sometimes prevails. However, the fact remains that what feels good at the time a decision is made is likely to be a major deciding factor. Whether we make a snap decision or take ages to settle on what to do, the real question in all this is, what is it that makes for that good feeling?

The practice of imagery involves using a premeditated mental process to achieve chosen goals. To do this we begin with the intellect and build on it. The intellect remains a great asset with which to set our major goals, but it would be ideal if we could complement it with a deeper wisdom.

While some people seem to have a natural wisdom that flows effortlessly, most of us experience our innate wisdom sporadically. So, how can we train and develop our inner wisdom and draw on its potential when we need to review or set goals? And can we do this in a way that leaves us happy with the goal, knowing that an inner 'good feeling' will give us the confidence to follow through and trust in the outcome.

There are three major possibilities or techniques for clarifying your goals.

1. Meditation and goal setting

One of the most common benefits people notice and describe to me when they begin meditation is that decisions now seem easier to make. They feel more confident of what they decide to do and these decisions actually do work better for them in the full context of their lives.

Barry was a reasonably successful small businessman who came to learn meditation with a desperate sense of needing to control stress. He was sleeping poorly, he was irritable and felt a constant nagging unease that he came to know as a vague, widespread but ill-defined fear. Barry began to meditate, and each time I saw him his smile became easier, more constant and wider. He reported with amazement how the fear just seemed to be melting. He could not say what was happening to it, as he was not addressing it directly. Neither was he sure where it was going, but he was sure it was going! In its place was a new-found confidence that warmed his smile. He was deeply impressed with the change in his decision-making—gone were the anxieties and doubts and now it seemed so easy. The results were delightful. Within a short space of time, his business improved so dramatically he won a major small business award.

Why then would meditation help goal setting? If you are affected by stress, it is almost certain you will be under-reacting or over-reacting. Stress clouds judgement. Tension creates strain and depletes energy. Meditation, on the other hand, helps you to regain a more natural state of balance and frees you to act appropriately. Meditation leads to a clear state of mind and allows wisdom to flow. So, without addressing the issues specifically, the regular practise of meditation can lead to the clarity of mind that facilitates good decision making.

However, if you prefer to be more actively involved in the conscious process of decision making, and choose to add to the benefits of passive meditation, there are two more specific techniques that can be recommended.

plation

on, or Insight Meditation, is an age-old
ed for problem solving, goal setting and for
gaining insight. I wrote a good deal about it, and how
to do it, in a major section of *Peace of Mind*. Here let us
summarise how to use contemplation in the context of
goal setting.

So we can investigate how this technique works, let
us use the example of reviewing your eating habits and
deciding on what sort of diet to follow. Here are the
steps.

Goal setting using contemplation

1. Decide what the issue is (e.g. our sample case,
   to set dietary goals) and determine to reach a
   conclusion.

2. Do the research. Use your intellect. Selectively
   explore the internet, read the books, speak to
   the experts, discuss it with friends, listen to
   CDs. Ideally make notes. This person said that,
   this book the other, etc. With food it is usually
   easiest to write lists of the different recommendations.

3. Set a time for the decision to be made. There
   are two ways to do this. If you were to buy a
   new washing machine, probably you would
   wait until you gathered all the relevant
   information. Presuming you have determined
   your price range, you could collect the details
   on all the makes and models available within a

reasonable period of time. However, with food you could collect information indefinitely. So you probably need to say to yourself something like 'I will collect all the information I can in the next two weeks (this two weeks is just an arbitrary figure I have used—there is no need to take me literally on this one – choose your own timeframe) and then I will make the best decision I can.'

4. On the day when the decision is to be made, give yourself some time – half an hour to an hour is ideal – and some space either where you meditate regularly or in any quiet area. Make sure you can be free from the telephone and other possible distractions. Take with you any notes you have made and any other material you have gathered. Also take a pen and some paper in case you want to write on it.

5. When you sit down, begin by reviewing your research material and in this way refresh all the knowledge you have of your subject. If you do not have all the written material go straight to the next step.

6. Consciously relax your body and calm your mind. This will be a familiar process if you have some experience of meditation. The aim is to relax as best you can so you are in a better state of mind to progress into the contemplation. If this is new to you and you want more help to relax now, you can follow the details on pages

93-103 of this book, or have a more complete introduction by reading Meditation – an In-depth Guide.

7. Once relaxed in this manner, focus your attention on consciously reviewing the facts as you remember them.

In our example, you might recall the style of food you have been eating, the broad issues relating to why you are considering changing your diet, what different people have recommended to you, what you have read in different books and so on.

If at any stage you become distracted or your mind wanders off onto other thoughts, as soon as you recognise this, be gentle with yourself and simply come back to concentrating on issues relating to food and diet.

This first part of the process then is clearly a rational, left brain exercise. You actively think about the topic and all issues relating to it. What happens next, as you continue to concentrate on the topic, is that at some point your mind will automatically shift into more abstract, intuitive, right brain contemplation. It will be as if all the facts you have been reflecting upon and analysing, all the pieces of the jigsaw puzzle as it were, come together and now you can clearly see the bigger picture. This will give you a new sense of comprehension and understanding and usually leaves you with a clear sense of what to do. This can all come with a moment of clear insight, almost like an 'Ah ha! I've got it' moment of revelation.

The more you practise this technique, the more reliable it becomes. It is a wonderful and dependable way to solve problems, develop creativity and instigate lateral thinking. As another aside, this is an excellent way to prepare for and complete creative writing.

8. Once the sense of clarity dawns, usually it is best to write the ensuing insight down. Perhaps you can remember having the experience of a moment of insight like this before. Perhaps you were in the shower or was it when you were half asleep, and suddenly like a bolt out of the blue, it seemed as if you have the perfect solution to a problem you had been wrestling with. Yet by the time you got dressed and ate breakfast, it had flown from your memory! Contemplation sometimes can be like that too, so it is best to write it down. I always do this exercise with pen and paper close by and as soon as the answer begins to form, write it down.

This contemplation technique can be used to solve any problem. It leads to a clarity that is backed by a deep sense of your own inner wisdom. As a result, the directions that come with it, the goals that emerge from this exercise, will feel very 'right' for you.

People often ask me "how can I trust the result of an

exercise like this?" Well, if you come out of this exercise with no clarity and are still clouded by doubt; all that has happened is you have spent time simply thinking about the issue. No harm done, but no insight either! The insight we are talking of has as one of its features the confidence of certainty. It comes with a deep inner knowing which is connected to that 'gut feeling' we talked of earlier. With this inner knowing there is no doubt. No one else will need to confirm such an insight for you; it will be easy to feel confident about, easy to commit to and it is highly likely to work well!

Now for another imagery exercise that is even more creative!

3. Inner Wisdom (or Inner Guide) imagery

This is an exercise we have found to be profoundly useful and effective in our retreat programs. In that setting, having taken time out from the busyness and distractions of daily life, and with the support of trained staff, many people have gained major insights through this process. Also, this is an exercise many have used effectively at home.

First, a little background. Scientifically, it is widely recognised that everything we ever learnt or experienced is stored in our memory. While a few rare individuals have what we call photographic memories with virtually total recall, most of us struggle a bit with better or worse memories. The good news, however, is that it is all in there. The only question is how to gain access to it.

You may have had some experience of being confronted with a major problem that almost demanded a solution, yet you were not quite sure what to do. Or perhaps there was the sense of having the answer to an elusive question 'on the tip of your tongue'-a sense of the solution being there, inside somewhere, but just out of reach! You may have had the experience of working hard for the solution, researching, questioning, reading, reflecting. All to no avail until almost in frustration you let it all go. Perhaps you were having a shower, walking in a park, or in that gentle reverie half way between being asleep and awake. Then POW! It almost seems to hit you and there it is – the answer, so simple, so obvious, so clear! Most of us have had this experience at some time in our lives, yet for most of us, this process occurs infrequently and somewhat unpredictably.

The following Inner Wisdom Imagery exercise aims to provide a structured way into that same level of wisdom, insight and clarity. And it also has a more pro-found possibility. A common psychological theory, made particularly popular by Carl Jung, is that there is a collec-tive unconscious. Just as we have our own inner wisdom accumulated by our range of personal experience, there is a vast body or reservoir of collective human experience. The theory is that this is like a mainframe computer with all the experience of the ages stored in it. Our own mind is like a PC that has its own individual memory, along with the potential to tap into the larger unit. You may quite reasonably question the truth of all this, but the delightful thing about meditation in general, and this Inner Wisdom Imagery exercise in particular, is that it provides you with a means to investigate the proposition and find out the truth of the matter for yourself.

The feature of this Inner Wisdom exercise is that when it works, as it does often, the responses you get, the insights it provides, will have a certainty that can only be gained through direct experience. As with the previous exercise, if you do this one and need to question whether the answers you receive are valid and real or not, then do question them deeply. For it is possible to do this exercise in the sense of wish fulfilment, to keep it on the emotional/rational level and get from it what you had hoped for or expected in a fairly superficial way.

The real opportunity with this exercise is to go beyond the rational thinking mind, to connect more directly with your unconscious and your own wisdom mind and perhaps even go beyond all this, and connect with the vast collective unconscious. Answers that come from that place come with a certainty beyond the need for questioning. They come with an assured sense of knowing. Often when this happens, major insights occur that can help you to understand more of your life, why you are like you are and what you can do to effectively manage major issues affecting your life.

What we are aiming to do then is to connect the conscious mind with the unconscious in a way the two can communicate. As we know already there is a common language which links the conscious and unconscious minds and that common language is imagery.

Using this knowledge, the aim of the Inner Wisdom Imagery exercise is to create in our mind an image that represents our unconscious inner wisdom – an image which our conscious mind can then communicate with, asking it questions, seeking and gaining answers.

The Inner Wisdom technique involves two steps. First we create an 'inner sanctuary' – an image we form in our mind of a place where we feel particularly peaceful and comfortable. This part of the exercise is often referred to as the Quiet Place. Creating this Quiet Place relaxes us, puts our mind at ease and transports us to an inner world where we are in more direct contact with the unconscious.

Then, into this Quiet Place we invite an image to join us – an image that will represent our inner wisdom. This image can take many forms; it is like an Inner Guide. For some it may be an archetypal old man with long white hair and beard and flowing robes, for others, Mother Mary, a saint or spirited figure from another tradition. For some, a special person in their life who has died, for others, an animal or a bird, domesticated or wild. There have been cartoon characters, rocks, even formless clouds with a powerful sense of presence that people have used to great effect as their Inner Guides.

The best way to approach this exercise is with the open and attentive mind of experimentation. While it is useful to have any questions you may have for your inner wisdom clear in your mind at the start, it is best to let go of any expectations as to what the outcome of the exercise will be. Very often, when you enter into this process fully and with an open mind, completely new images, questions and directions can arise spontaneously.

Take time to relax and calm your mind first, then follow the exercise and be interested to notice what happens.

The Inner Wisdom Imagery exercise

1. Begin by taking time to clarify your question. If you have an obvious issue or problem for which you need a creative solution, simply formulate it into a question. Perhaps you could also ponder what question you would ask if you were able to speak directly to your inner wisdom – what would that question be?

2. Give yourself the space and time for the exercise – about half an hour is enough, although it is helpful if you have more time available so that when you finish you can simply relax and reflect on the exercise if you choose to.

3. The exercise can be done lying down, but if it is easy for you, it is preferable to sit upright on a chair or on the floor.

4. Take a few moments to consciously relax your body a little in whatever way works best for you.

5. Now allow an image to form in your mind of a place where you feel particularly peaceful and comfortable. It may be a place you have been to before; or it may be a fantasy place. Just allow an image to form in your mind of a place where you feel particularly peaceful and comfortable – and in a way that you can explore it in more detail.

   Notice firstly where this Quiet Place is. Is it a fantasy place, a composite of several places you

know, or one specific place? Be reminded there
is no right or wrong in this, just concentrate on
this place, which is special for you.

Now what can you see in this place? What
is close by? What shapes, what sizes, what
colours? What shades of colours? Take your
time to enjoy looking at the details, building
them up steadily. You will probably notice
what time of day it is. If you can see the sky,
are there clouds, or is it clear? You probably
will also notice if there is any movement or
if it is quite still. Really *notice* the details as
fully as you can.

Now *listen* for what sounds you can hear in this
place. What can you hear nearby or are there
any sounds coming from further away? What
sounds can you hear in this place?

Give your attention to noticing what you may
be able to smell in this place – what fragrance,
what odour, what can you smell in this place?
You will probably be able to *feel* the temperature in this place. Is it warm or cool, or is it
neutral? Can you feel any breeze on your skin,
or the warmth of the sun on you face? Notice
too your position and what you have contact
with – is it hard or soft, damp or dry? So,
notice what physical sensations go with this
place.

Be aware that if there is anything you would
prefer to change to make this place even more
peaceful and comfortable, you could do that.

Now dwell on the *feeling* that comes with being in this place. Allow these feelings to build within you and rest with those feelings for a few moments.

6. Imagine that off in the distance a small white cloud or mist is forming and that it begins to move slowly towards you. There is a knowing that within this cloud will be a symbol that represents your Inner Wisdom, your Inner Guide. As the small cloud moves closer to you, the shape of the symbol begins to form and becomes clearly obvious. The symbol may then move out of the cloud and approach you, coming to within a comfortable distance. This is your Inner Guide.

   Notice the features of your Inner Guide. Notice what size it is, taking in the details. Perhaps your Inner Guide has a name that you seem to know already, or you could ask for it. Is there something you would like to say to your Inner Guide? Perhaps, there is a question? If so, then ask it. Again, expect a reply. You may hear that reply as clearly as any conversation, or it may come as an inner knowing. Either way, it may lead to an exchange or a conversation.

   Or perhaps your Inner Guide has something to say to you, perhaps a question for you? You could listen for that.

7. When you feel ready to take your leave, perhaps there is something you would like to

do or something you would like to say before
you go? Perhaps some contact, perhaps some
more words, perhaps an arrangement to meet
again? Perhaps a sense of this Inner Guide, this
Inner Wisdom remaining close to you with
ready access?

8. Once you have parted, bring your attention
   back to your Quiet Place, your inner sanctuary. Take a few moments to feel yourself in
   that special place once again. Then probably
   you will be aware of a part of this place that
   appeals to you most particularly. If you are
   not there already, go to that place so you can
   rest a while. Lie down, and as you do so, feel
   your body relaxing completely, so much so
   that you feel almost as if you could float up a
   little off the ground, just resting now for a few
   moments, floating just a few inches off
   the ground.

9. When you are ready you can begin to end the
   exercise. Be reminded that at any time you
   choose to in the future you can return to this
   exercise, and that each time you do it will be
   easier and even more complete.
   Now bring your attention back to your body.
   Feel your toes move a little, move your hands
   a little, perhaps a deeper breath or two, and
   when you are ready, let your eyes gently
   open again.

This exercise often leads to major insights and deeply satisfying answers. It can be used regularly or simply when you have a particular need. It may be helpful to read the extra details on how to start this exercise by developing and using the Quiet Place Imagery in Chapter Eight.

While for many people this is an exercise that is straightforward, easy and deeply satisfying, the range of experiences does vary. For some it is a bit of a non-event while for a small few it can lead to images that initially are confusing or disconcerting. These images, although difficult or confronting at first can be very useful in their own right. There are a number of ways to effectively deal with difficult images and while this is covered in Chapter Seven, another reminder here. If you feel you need help, you would be wise to seek professional help or call on the Gawler Foundation's qualified staff.

What follows is a particularly dramatic example of this Inner Wisdom Imagery at work. It highlights how often the images have to be worked on to begin with, almost as if the initial images are 'manufactured' or invoked. However, frequently there is then the sense of fully entering into the exercise, in a very real and meaningful way.

When it came to imagery exercises, Kerry was one of those people who had difficulty forming clear images. When she began the inner wisdom imagery exercise, she experienced a very hazy Quiet Place and really struggled to find any image for her Inner Wisdom. As I began to help her directly, a symbolic image of a golden triangle formed. It was filled with a great deal of light. When prompted, Kerry asked this symbol her question 'Where do I find love?' There was a long pause and a disappointed

'No answer.'

Sensing there was a block to all this, I suggested Kerry might like to ask 'Who do I have to forgive?' She felt good with this and asked the question of her inner wisdom. The answer came straight back with total clarity, 'Yourself.'

Prompting Kerry again, I suggested she might like to ask what she needed to forgive herself for. Again she did this and put the question to her Inner Guide, the golden triangle. Another immediate response: 'For being alive!' This came like a thunderbolt to Kerry. It was so power-ful and touched such a deep note of recognition in the core of her being that she became very emotional, almost hysterical.

Almost immediately another image came into her awareness. At first it was of herself as a child, then an even earlier image and feeling that was of the time when she was in her mother's womb before she was born. These images were arising quite spontaneously now. Kerry was simply describing them to me as they formed. She explained that she had a very strong feeling her mother had not wanted her and she did not feel welcome to be born.

Later Kerry explained to me that during the time her mother was pregnant with the unborn Kerry, her mother had separated from her father. Kerry's mother already had two small children, aged one and two, and had needed to return to the family home for the birth. Her parents were strict Catholics and deeply disappointed by the thought of the separation and their daughter having a child with no father present.

What this exercise did for Kerry was to help her make sense of why she had become the woman she had. She realised that she had been apologising all her life for simply being here: apologising for being alive! Now, through the exercise she realised that it was OK to be alive and that she did deserve to be here.

Kerry also came to realise her mother had done the best she could at the time. But she was aware that as a child all of this had been fairly awful and affected her life deeply. Now, as an adult, she knew she could change. The exercise had clarified some profound issues and given her the goal of actually reclaiming her life.

Kerry went on to work hard at forgiving her mother and now, years later, feels she can love her as her mother. She still finds that as a person her mother is difficult to be with and there is ongoing work to do. For herself, Kerry found this one imagery exercise quite transformational having completely reframed a core inner belief. What it did was to leave her feeling more optimistic, joyful, peaceful and yes, alive!

The Inner Wisdom exercise is useful for tackling the big questions. Some people do use it on simpler, day to day issues, while most find that for more straightforward goal setting needs, the earlier two techniques are often more relevant. Taken together, the hope is these three goal setting exercises are as useful for you as they are for most.

Let us now consider more of the key principles that can be used to make your imagery fully effective. The next step involves considering the point from which we will start.

CHAPTER 5

POSITIVE THINKING 101 –
Acknowledge where you are starting from.

T HE MIND AS we have discovered already, is a goal orientated, decision-making tool. When it comes to how we use the mind, it is a bit like following a map. You decide upon a destination, a goal. Fixing that goal in mind, you then make a range of choices that appear most likely to lead you to your destination. Along the way, you are quite likely to come to crossroads, diversions and obstacles as well as tranquil, easy stretches. You check your position, you get feedback, assess your progress, make any corrections, refocus on your goal. All this makes for a useful metaphor.

However, think back to the obvious. When you look up a map, say a street map to find your way across town, before you can begin the journey you need two very important locations. Normally we think first of the end point, the destination, the goal. But before you can actually begin the journey, you need to know where you are starting from!

This seems to me to be a point often overlooked by people engaged in so called positive thinking. 'So called', because while it does involve being positive, it also involves acknowledging the starting point – where you are right now. Presuming you feel the need to be some-where else, presuming you want to use positive thinking to move to a new place, to be different, to be better, to be healthier, happy, wealthier, whatever; it follows there is at least some sense that where you are now is not satisfactory. Mindfulness may be about accepting where you are, but positive thinking is something else. This is the joy and the power of positive thinking and imagery: it can facilitate major personal change and be used with great creative power to set new goals, achieve them and enhance many aspects of life.

Yet many people who embark on all this, attempt to gloss over their current problems.

There seems to have been a prevailing view amongst many in the community that to be positive you are not allowed even a whiff of what we might commonly call a negative emotion. Tears, grief, anger, sadness, rage – all these so-called negative emotions seem to have pretty poor press amongst many 'positive thinkers'.

In my experience, failing to acknowledge where you are starting from, and feeling the emotion of that place works for only a small minority. For some, perhaps those people who are rigid or strong in their thinking – left brained, analytical and logical – it can work. For most, however, omitting or neglecting this step of acknowledg-ment leads to a sense of denial; denial that may be helpful for a short while, but often leads to a breakdown and a need to reassess and start again.

The best example that comes to mind to illustrate this point concerns a delightful couple I met interstate. We had arranged to conduct one of our residential cancer self help programs in Perth and this Sydney couple flew across to join it, as they were quite desperate. The husband, Martin had been diagnosed six weeks earlier with bowel cancer and liver secondaries. He had been happily married to his wife Joyce for over forty years and for much of that time they had worked together; by all accounts in a very happy relationship. A little over a year previously, Martin had been badly betrayed by his business partner and he internalised all his anger, grief and despair. Martin felt sure in himself that the way he reacted to this major stress had been a precipitating factor in his illness. At the same time he acknowledged he had lived a somewhat extravagant lifestyle and was not surprised the bowel was where his disease showed up.

Joyce had been deeply affected by her husband's diagnosis and she was determined to be the ideal support person for Martin. Joyce loved Martin dearly and was ready to do whatever she could to help. Her idea of what this meant was she needed to maintain a stiff upper lip, hold her own emotions in and exude an outer, positive manner.

So, for six weeks most of Joyce's energy had been going into attempting to hold her tears back. She felt heartbroken with what had happened, and was deeply shocked by the doctor's dire predictions for the man she loved. Keeping up a brave face was hard work.

By the time Joyce and Martin's plane landed in Perth and they began to make their way to our program, Joyce said she could feel her knees starting to wobble nervously. As the group began and people made their introductions, it was obvious both Joyce and Martin were making huge efforts to contain their emotions.

At the end of the second day Joyce approached me and said she felt she really needed to leave the course, book into a motel, wait until the program was over and then return to collect Martin. In response to my obvious inquiry, she explained she feared if she stayed any longer she would be completely unable to contain her emotions. She was truly fearful that if she let them out she would open the floodgates, crying uncontrollably and unceasingly and cry alot. Her real concern, she said, was not for her, but for what impact her emotions would have on Martin. She did not want to appear negative around him; she only wanted to be positive so she could best help him.

It was easy to agree with her on the value of being positive. Then I put it to her that if I had been married to her for over forty years in what I had thought had been a happy marriage, and if I had been diagnosed with a rather nasty form of cancer with a poor medical prognosis, and faced with all of this she showed no emotion, I would wonder what I really meant to her, what had gone wrong? I explained to Joyce her emotional reaction to Martin's diagnosis was very natural and reasonable. Sure, it is true that occasionally partners do react without tears. However, I suspect this is rather rare, and Joyce's response is more the norm. Importantly, that is not to say one is right or wrong

– but clearly the reactions are very different.

It seems to me there are two issues here. The first is the natural response to the situation- the problem as I would call it. Some may prefer to call it a challenge or an opportunity; to my simple mind it sure sounds at this stage like a bloody problem! It may be reframed to become a challenge or an opportunity, and that is what I would hope for and expect, but let us deal with what it is like to begin with first. There is the immediate reaction to the problem, then there is this judgemental part of our mind that comes in and comments on whether that reaction is reasonable or not. In Joyce's case, her assessment was that showing her emotions was not acceptable or in Martin's best interests. I explained to her the problem now was not that she was upset- the problem was that she was upset with being upset.

Joyce acknowledged all of this and then said she feared that if she started to cry, she may never stop. I reassured her that she was bound to stop sooner or later. I was right – it only took three days! When given permission, Joyce's tears began to fall like spring rain – soft, steady and fairly continuous. Once she started, Martin joined in and between them they still hold our record for the most tissues used in a program! With no outside pressures or distractions, and surrounded by others who had a genuine and compassionate understanding of where they were at, Joyce and Martin shared their grief.

At the end of the program, Joyce made a point of thanking the group for providing them with a safe space and for supporting them through that time. She said that now she felt as if a huge weight had been lifted from her shoulders. She acknowledged there may well be times in the future when she would cry again, but never with the same intensity and always with a new-found ease and sense of appropriateness. Joyce told us all she felt wonderful, as now she did not need to waste her energy attempting to contain her feelings. Now she was free to put her energy into supporting and caring for Martin.

This is acknowledging where you are at, where you are starting from. Once this is done, in the way that works and is complete for you, then you are free to move on. If you have any doubt about how you are going with this issue, it may well be worthwhile to discuss it with a trusted friend or member of the family, or perhaps go to a counsellor to make sure you are travelling well.

Do be warned there is the potential trap for some people of becoming stuck in the expression of the painful emotions. What is desirable is full acknowledgment and expression, then to be encouraged in the ability to move on – moving on to learn what to do about it all and putting all of this into practise.

For the next step, let us consider three practical principles that enable us to move on and to develop and use imagery effectively.

CHAPTER 6

THREE PRACTICAL PRINCIPLES –
Key criteria for effective imagery

As was pointed out in the first chapter, imagery techniques can be learnt and applied with little depth of understanding and they still may work quite well. However, the more you understand what you are doing, why what you are doing works and how, the more power you give to it. Having studied and developed the theory behind imagery in the second chapter, what can we say about the best way to apply the techniques?

When it comes to the effective practise of imagery, the images we use need to be:

1. accurate
2. complete
3. accompanied by a strong feeling.

Each of these three principles is essential for the successful practise of imagery. The more fully we can accomplish each of the three, the quicker and more effectively our imagery will work. We are about to investigate what each point really means and we will refer back to these essentials as the different forms of imagery are detailed throughout the book.

It will be helpful to be aware that when many people begin to use imagery exercises, there are elements of their images that are inaccurate, incomplete or do not feel good. This is a particularly important issue in Healing Imagery, but is relevant to all aspects of imagery use. Why this happens, why initial images often have limitations, is that while consciously you may have a clear intention, a clear goal, unconsciously you may well have your doubts or fears. Remember, imagery is the language of the unconscious mind and when practising imagery we are involving and activating this part of our being. So, it would not be surprising for any negativity we hold internally to be mirrored in the images we form.

While in one sense this is a worry, particularly if we do not realise the problem, in a more important sense imagery provides an excellent opportunity to bring any negativity to conscious awareness, to recognise it, address it and transform it. This is another powerful strength of imagery –it can be used in this highly creative, personally therapeutic way.

In this chapter we will begin by examining the positive side of imagery and what ideally that means. Then we will need to look more deeply into the darker side of the so called negative or scary images and learn how we deal with them.

1. Effective images need to be accurate

The need for the images you use to be accurate probably

seems obvious enough.

The mind functions using imagery as its language and operates much like a computer.

The old 'garbage in, garbage out' principle certainly applies, so if you give your mind vague, indecisive or inaccurate images to work with, there will be little or no result.

The mind is goal-orientated; it likes clear goals and once it has one, it will do its best to implement that goal, irrespective of whatever type of goal that happens to be. Importantly, the mind does not discriminate when it comes to using imagery. It will do its best to fulfil a goal whether it be destructive or constructive. Therefore the imperative to get your images right remains with the initiator of the image. Once the image has been chosen and activated, the mind will support it with the full force of its creative power.

A classic healing example of the need for accuracy involved a young boy with cancer who was having chemotherapy. He was hoping to use the image of two warplanes to empower his treatment. When asked to draw all this, he drew two planes attacking head on, each firing bullets at the other. One plane represented the cancer, the other the treatment. In the drawing, however, when the lines of bullets were extended, the bullets from the chemotherapy plane missed the cancer plane, while the cancer planes bullets went directly into the chemotherapy. In other words, the boy was reflecting his inner belief that the cancer was stronger than the chemotherapy, and that he expected the treatment to do little good.

I guess you could go into all sorts of in-depth analysis

with all this. However, in my experience all the boy needs is to be told to shoot straight! This is related to the fact that while unconscious beliefs can affect the nature of the images we form, the reverse is also true. Imagery can be used in a highly creative, personally therapeutic way to change deeply held unconscious beliefs. This is an exciting field of therapeutic work and it offers real possibilities for personal development as we will discover throughout this book.

How then can you be sure your images are accurate? One of the best ways is to draw them. You can make just one drawing to represent your imagery at work; or do what many do and draw a series of 'cartoons' that set out in more detail what your imagery involves. Then find a counsellor or valued friend you trust. Explain to them what your intention is with your imagery and then show them the drawing(s) you have made, and ask for their feedback. With a trained counsellor this can be a very valuable exercise, while even a perceptive friend is likely to notice any glaring inconsistencies. As the drawing is a reflection of your own state of mind, it is common that initially you may not notice what may have seemed with the benefit of hindsight to have been obvious inaccuracies.

So while being accurate is a key issue in imagery, these solutions also relate to the next point – your imagery needs to be complete.

2. Using images that are complete

That the images be complete is another crucial factor which often comes into creative and positive thinking. In my very early days of learning and using these principles, I had a friend Geoff who was even more convinced of these principles than I, and he used imagery techniques regularly. Geoff was on a real spiritual journey in his life and very deeply committed to living his truth.

A business opportunity arose which was highly ethical and which would lead to genuine benefits for many people. To take up this rare opportunity, Geoff needed $10,000! This all occurred long enough ago for that to be quite a deal of money. Having been preoccupied with his spiritual life, Geoff had no cash or assets, although he was well educated and highly talented. So he had a genuine need and decided to test his principles.

Geoff imagined receiving the $10,000 and affirmed receiving it, using accurate imagery. (This is a true story.) Quite suddenly and unexpectedly. his father died. In his will, you can probably guess, he left Geoff exactly $10,000 – no more, no less! A remarkable coincidence? Who knows, but there was no doubting what happened was quite remarkable.

I took the lesson from this that to be complete, often it is wise to add in, almost as a proviso, 'in a harmonious way.' Perhaps it is being judgemental to suggest Geoff's father's death was not harmonious. In some ways it perfectly met a genuine need and Geoff's project did help many people! Perhaps it was all as it was meant to be. I know initially Geoff was deeply disturbed by the 'coincidence' and it caused both of us a great deal of introspection and reflection.

Another example of this principle of being complete is that I have heard of cancer patients who have used highly aggressive imagery to attack their cancer. Some have succeeded in becoming cured physically and yet I have been told some of these people who used aggression have become so aggressive and unpleasant in their own personality it would be hard to say real healing took place.

To be complete here, the imagery certainly does need to be accurate and effective in the physical sense. However, it is quite possible to achieve this end while aiming to bring about peace and harmony in the emotional, mental and spiritual spheres as well. These issues will be discussed more fully in Chapters Twelve and Thirteen.

3. Empowering imagery with feelings

The degree of emotion or feeling, and the amount of passion that accompanies imagery, provides a major key to explain the difference between imagery that leads to little or no effect, and that which brings about dramatic results. Passion is a high energy state and is by definition a strong emotion that generates enthusiasm and commitment.

It seems clear that emotion drives imagery. It is emotion that converts a casual thought into a stimulus for action. For example, in the field of medicine, Candace Pert was the first research scientist to set out the physical mechanisms whereby thoughts influence the way the body functions through the agency of emotion. Her ground breaking book of 1997, *Molecules of Emotion* is highly recommended if you seek an accessible, yet detailed science-based introduction to this key aspect of Mind-Body Medicine – how emotion is a necessity when we seek to actively influence our capacity for healing and wellbeing.

What experience tells us is that in any field of endeavour, in any arena where we use imagery, emotion leads to enthusiasm, which in turn leads to its companions: determination, resilience and perseverance. Emotion then, is an essential part of effective imagery, and strong emotion, or passion, is therefore likely to be most potent and the ideal to aim for. The only question is what type of passion works best – common old ordinary passion or altruistic passion?

No doubt everyone can remember having a passion for something in their life. Something you really felt for, loved or were committed to. Something you just naturally were prepared to do whatever it took to achieve. My hope is you were able to follow it through. Passion fulfilled is a true delight and can propel us to accomplish great things.

Often I work with people who in fairness would say thwarted passion was behind their illness. Not only am I talking of thwarted love here, although that may well be the issue, but any passion in life that was blocked, put aside, overwhelmed by the busyness of life or just simply put off and forgotten – these are the lost passions that can lead to illness. These are the passions that when remembered and rekindled lead back to life and joy- preventing illness if it has not arrived already. It is passion that often sparks radical healing when it is required.

To understand passion more fully, and to realise how to develop and sustain it, next we need to examine the two types of passion that are most relevant to how we use and train the mind.

Altruistic Passion – Compassion

Altruistic passion is the result of a pure motive based upon spiritual clarity. This type of passion is characterised by three things: 'Right seeing', 'Right motive', 'Right action'. It is founded upon unconditional love.

Right seeing is a state of clarity: the state of clear thinking resulting from a wisdom-based understanding of whatever the problem or the issues may be.

Right motive is based upon compassion for all, and is a state where there is a commitment to the best outcome for all. It is not a bargain such as 'I will go back to Church if I get the new job!' Compassion is the urge to help others to be free of suffering and commonly it leads to a level of commitment that has a unconditional quality about it that can be likened to devotion. True spiritual devotion is unconditional. True devotion is an uncomplicated state where the commitment has a spiritual focus. While commonly this occurs in the context of a religious tradition, many are capable of making this type of commitment in a more abstract way; committing themselves to basic spiritual principles and pursuing an ethical or spiritually-based life. Pure, heartfelt devotion has a very powerful, very clear energy behind it that empowers all it touches. This is the basis of altruism.

Right action is free from the stress of over-reacting or under-reacting, it is simply doing the right thing at the right time. Right action involves doing what is required in a focussed, resolute and calmly determined manner. This attitude has the atmosphere of the true martial arts and is a state developed through practices such as meditation, mindfulness and spiritual discipline. It may not be as flamboyant or exciting as the base passions, but there is a calm, an ease and a grace about this state that is heartwarming to be around. It is an incredibly powerful state.

Ordinary or Base Passion

But does the feeling accompanying imagery need to be so altruistic? Will any strong feeling fire effective imagery? What of good old fashioned hate, lust, greed and revenge? No doubt we all have our share of those feelings from time to time. Here is where it gets really interesting and perhaps I have to speculate, as research is going on rapidly in this field.

We can all observe the power that negative or destructive emotions have to fuel personal gain. Looking around there seems to be plenty of evidence that anger, greed, revenge etc. bring short-term gains. Perhaps if physical wealth was the only issue, these emotions would be lauded. Yet looking deeper, the sad human cost of these rampant emotions is heavy indeed.

It is a major tenet of Buddhism that base passions provide the root cause of suffering: anger, attachment, pride and jealousy – all base passions which sooner of later backfire on us at heavy cost. So to heal the heart, to overcome base passions and to aspire to a more altruistic, compassionate view, this is an essential component of life itself. These lofty emotions are a vital aspect of any truly satisfying and sustaining practice of imagery. Key practices to assist with this are set out in Chapter Fifteen, Healing the Heart.

The special case of passion in healing

My own personal and clinical experience supports research in Mind-Body Medicine that demonstrates emotion plays a key role in the mind's ability to activate and direct physical healing. Here again the question – when it comes to healing, what type of emotion is most effective? Will powerful, fear-based emotions be effective, or are other motives more useful? What works best?

In the field of healing, it seems any strong emotion is more beneficial than none, at least in the short or often medium term.

After our cancer self help groups had been running a few years, we became aware of a dramatic study published in the world's foremost medical journal The Lancet. This study by Greer and Pettingale investigated the psychological reactions of women diagnosed with breast cancer, and the effect of these reactions on their survival. All the woman were found to have reacted in one of four quite different ways. Some reacted with denial, pretending as if nothing had happened and attempting to bury their heads in the sand. Others came out with a fighting spirit, determined this illness was not going to beat them and they would do all possible to become survivors. The next group reacted with stoic acceptance, virtually saying in response to the question 'Why me?", "Why not! It's here, I guess I just have to put up with it." Finally there were those who responded with resignation, 'Things always go wrong for me, this is just another horrible example!'

After five years the survival rates of the four groups were markedly different. Perhaps not so surprisingly, the stoic acceptance and resignation groups had fared quite poorly and only 20 per cent were still alive in both groups. Also, perhaps not surprisingly to us at least, the women with a fighting spirit were doing exceptionally well, with 80 percent survival. But there was one big surprise. The women who were using denial also had an 80 percent survival rate!

At first this really puzzled the group of therapists I was working with. What did it mean? Why was it so? What should we do? Should we abandon teaching has to develop and activate a fighting spirit using self help techniques like meditation, imagery, diet and positive thinking? Maybe it would be as effective and quite a deal simpler to foster denial and discourage people from discussing their problems, sharing their feelings and experiences and actively seeking solutions?

We reflected on this deeply. Then it occurred to me. To react to a major illness such as breast cancer with denial is a very powerful emotional response! To do so would take quite a deal of energy. Remember most of these women would have had a breast surgically removed. To carry on as if nothing had happened, to use denial in the face of all that is a powerful reaction indeed!

So at the time we speculated these women would not be able to keep it up. Either they would have to change their tactics, or their energy would run out and problems re-emerge.

Another five years later, follow up results were published and again they were quite remarkable. The stoic acceptance and resignation groups had sadly nearly all died. The fighting spirit ladies were virtually all intact with still nearly 80 percent surviving. But now the denial

dropped off steadily to 50 per cent. After
years this decline continued to 20 per cent,
...e the fighting spirit women continued on.

So it may well be that strong emotions or strong reactions of any sort can fire healing in the short to medium term. However, it would seem it is the life affirming qualities, the ones we normally label as positive thinking and healthy emotions, that seem to lead to endurance – as well as happiness!

The fear of death, dying or disease obviously fuels strong emotions and can motivate people highly towards survival. This works well to begin with and it is with this emotion, this fear, that most people start. It is a natural response and provides a powerful incentive to get going. If it is where you are at, particularly if it is early days, there is nothing to worry about. However, if fear remains the motivational force, sooner or later it runs out, wears people out, becomes too hard. What does sustain people in the long term is a recognition of the preciousness of life and its wonderful possibilities. To switch from the fear of dying to a joyful, pure passion for life is one vital key that leads to long-term survival. More of this in the Healing Chapters.

The question of control

A final point to consider is that of the individual's sense of control. Feeling out of control in the normal sense of the word leads to feelings of hopelessness and helplessness. This undoubtedly blocks imagery and most other aspects of life. It certainly affects out health dramatically.

A somewhat unkind rat experiment very effectively

highlighted the impact that the sense of being in control can have. Similar rats were divided into three groups. The fortunate control group were left alone and their lives went on as normally as a laboratory rat's life goes on. The two experimental groups were placed in similar cages with similar conditions. The nasty bit was that the floors of their two cages were electrified. From time to time a mild electric current was switched on. The only way to turn it off was for one of the first group of rats to realise that pressing the magical buzzer in their cage did in fact switch it off. This had the bonus effect of switching off the second group's electrical shock as well.

The real sting in this experiment was the second group of rats did not know how it was all happening. The second group did not have a buzzer, nor could they see the other rats at work. In other words, the first group quickly learnt the electric shock came often enough but they could turn it off. They had a measure of control. The second group had no control; no sense of what was happening. They were subjected to the same amount of electricity, but for them it appeared to occur in a quite random manner that was completely beyond their control.

The outcome? All the rats had their immune function measured. For those with access to the control button their immunity initially dropped, indicating the stress was depleting them. However, after a while their immune function came up, rose above normal levels and remained elevated! It seemed being stressed, and then feeling able to overcome the stress – being able to feel in control – actually led to a heightening of the immune function in the first group of rats. The second group, the rats with no sense of control, simply died. Quickly. Once the electric shocks began, their immune function deteriorated in line with their counterparts who had access to the control button. But with no sense of control themselves, their immune function simply continued to fade away and they died.

There is no question that a sense of control is a key factor in health and wellbeing. Again, the question remains – what type of control works?

Phil was what is politely referred to as a control freak. An intellectual, domineering type, Phil was highly successful in work and sport. He worked hard, pushed himself, was fastidious with deadlines, always "on top of things". Then he developed cancer of the kidney. No problem. Change diet, learn to meditate, use imagery, even change jobs. Always in control. Tight, rigid, I can do it. I can achieve this. Go, go, go!

Then one day Phil woke up and all he could do was cry. No energy. No direction. Just a big black hole, a feeling of emptiness. Phil realised his will had run out. His ego-driven will had run out of push, run out of energy.

Phil spent three days in bed in the depths of despair. He felt lost, confused, totally deflated. For Phil it was his "long night of the soul"; that transformative pit in which all seems lost, until what you are really looking for is found. Phil found his spirit. In the depths of his despair, when all he had been familiar with seemed lost, Phil felt his essence – his spiritual essence. And in doing so he found an enthusiasm for life that came from a different place. Gone was the striving of the ego-driven will. In its place was a joyful enthusiasm, a sense of right action, a sense of honouring the sacredness in life by committing all his energy to healing – in body, mind and spirit. This led to a discipline that was easy and sustainable. While he continued to do many of the same things he was doing before the crisis, now he was doing them in a different state of mind. He was doing them with an assured ease, an inner commitment, an inner confidence. Phil went on to become a remarkable long-term survivor.

It would seem many people these days hope to use ego-based control to manage their lives, relying upon physical, emotional or mental energy. Their hope is to make their world secure. Unfortunately, this means they are placing their hopes for security on things that are inherently insecure – jobs, people, houses, banks. Clearly, all these things have the potential to change. They are what we call impermanent. Eventually they come and go. So what does give enduring security? What can we rely upon? What gives an enduring sense of being in control?

This security is the key element of the spiritual path. The recognition of the need to let go of the ego-based sense of control and to put our confidence in an enduring reality.

There are two options available that will help with this. The first is to build on a secure physical base, to meet our emotional needs and to educate our mind. From this security it is possible to launch into the spiritual life. In my experience only a few do it this way. My hope is that more will!

For many, however, just like Phil, this letting go, this transformation, only comes when a trauma or crisis initiates the second option, and takes us to the edge, to that point where our old methods and habits no longer work. At that point, the only choice we are left with is to let go and fly.

Like Phil, my own illness took me past my physical limits; it took me past my emotional and mental limits. In doing so it introduced me directly to the essence of who I really am. This direct experience gave me an unshakable trust in life itself, a joy for it, and a heartfelt commitment to helping others.

So here is another key benefit with imagery. It provides a powerful way to take back a sense of control. With imagery you have a means readily at your disposal that you can use to feel in control. While for many this control begins with its basis in the thinking, rational mind, we can aspire to higher motives through using the techniques in later chapters on Invocation, Manifestation and Healing the Heart.

Thus far we have been dwelling on the principles and basic techniques of imagery along with the limitations and the possibilities. Now we can get even more practical as we discuss and experiment with how to prepare our mind and body to get the best out of imagery, then we will learn how to practise imagery for specific purposes.

CHAPTER 7

THE PRELIMINARIES –
Preparing for effective imagery

Having completed some introductory imagery exercises already, and having dwelt on the principles behind imagery, you will be getting a taste for what this type of meditative practice is like. Before we go on to delve into more specific applications of imagery, let us clarify general issues relating to the practice – how to get started, when to do it, how often to do it – essentially, how to set it up so it will work best.

To be clear, imagery is a type of meditation practice. To receive the full benefits of this type of inner work it is very helpful to have the broader context gained from understanding the full scope of meditation. If you have not done so already, I recommend you commence by reading my book *Peace of Mind*. This provides an overview of the different types of meditation, a good deal of information on how to begin meditation and in the section on Creative Meditation contains quite some detail on imagery. In

Meditation – an In-depth Guide, there is valuable detail on how to relax your body, calm your mind, develop mindfulness and then let go into the deeper stillness of profound meditation. While the primary intention of *Meditation – an In-depth Guide* is to provide access to the heart and essence of meditation practice, the preliminary sections of this book are specifically relevant as a starting point for imagery. So do be encouraged to read these other books, although I will be summarising all that is essential for imagery in this chapter.

The point to emphasise over and over is that imagery is a dynamic, wilful, mind-generated activity. Imagery harnesses the power of the mind and as it has been said many times now, it has the potential to be destructive or creative.

One of the surest safeguards for imagery, one of the most reliable ways to ensure positive effects prevail, is to use imagery against the background of the regular practice of a specific type of meditation – mindfulness based stillness meditation (MBSM). This type of meditation (as described in detail in *Meditation – an In-depth Guide*) has four steps that are easy to learn and practice: preparation, relaxation, mindfulness and stillness. MBSM has many benefits and is highly recommended for your regular meditation practice. Of direct relevance to our discussion here, is that MBSM is aimed at regaining and sustaining a natural state of balance. If we are predominantly in balance ("predominantly" because health is regarded as a dynamic state of balance and life is bound to be attended by fluctuations), we will find there are many natural, almost automatic benefits.

The theory here is that when we are basically in a balanced state, many positive qualities find their natural expression. For example, it is natural to be positive, natural to be joyful, natural to be clear and confident. Interestingly, it is also natural to be mostly fearless. Babies are born with only two inherent fears – a fear of heights and a fear of loud noises. Any other fears we have to learn.

When we relax, let go and return to the natural balance of meditation, we can let go of acquired fears; just as we can let go of tension, anxiety and stress. If we do happen to be stressed, and sadly who is not these days (unless they have been doing something to let it go already), then we tend to over-react or under-react, neither of which is conducive to confident and effective imagery practice.

For all these reasons then, it is wise to meditate regularly using the MBSM method and to be aware you are supporting your imagery in this way.

Given the benefits of MBSM, which is what could be described as a 'passive' form of meditation where the aim is to calm and still the mind, and given that imagery very much involves using the mind in an active and dynamic way, many people ask me which is better, which should I do – meditation or imagery?

While this is a book on imagery, I would have to say that for daily, regular practice, if you were only to do one thing, I would recommend the passive, silent form of MBSM. The sustained benefits of a little time spent each day in a state of deep natural balance are profound. However, the imagery techniques we have been investigating so far, and will be discussing and practising further, do have exceptional, specific benefits. So I prefer to think of combining the various practices, keeping the simple MBSM for the regular routine, and using imagery when the specific needs are there. Many people have benefited from learning a range of imagery techniques and from having them available for use when required. I heartily recommend this approach.

The right attitude

Already, we have discussed in some detail the importance of the attitude with which you approach your imagery practice. Again, to reiterate, ideally you do imagery in a state of mind that is clear, confident and calm. It may well be, however, that when you first start a new type of imagery exercise, or apply imagery to a new problem or need, you are far from the ideal of being clear, confident and calm! It may well be that the exercise, the imagery practice you do, helps in itself to lead you into a more relaxed state where you can regain your sense of ease, and so the practice itself helps you directly in becoming more confident.

So, understand the ideals put forward in this book are just what they are – ideals. Recognise that perfecting any ideal is almost fanciful – yet ideals give a very useful sense of direction. They point towards what to do, and any step you take towards fulfilling an ideal is well worthwhile.

For example, there is no doubt that as an ideal it is recommended to be relaxed. Yet relaxation is not a black and white event – there is a sliding scale from fully tense to fully relaxed. A major principle here is that if you do an exercise that relaxes you seventy per cent, make sure you delight in being seventy per cent more relaxed than when you started, rather than being stressed by the thirty per cent you are away from total relaxation.

Be gentle with yourself. And also be smart too. Each time you practise imagery, there are important preliminaries that will assist you to be well prepared and ready to get full benefit from your efforts.

Preparing for effective creative imagery

1. Prepare your outer environment

Consider how you can arrange the space where you do your practice, so it supports you best. Ideally minimise all external distractions so you can concentrate fully on this inner work. Deal with the telephone, take your leave from others in the house.

It can be helpful to regularly use the same place for your practice. Make it special with photographs, special objects, flowers and decorations. Many find lighting a candle adds a special atmosphere.

2. Prepare your inner environment

We have spent a good deal of time already clarifying that the ideal inner environment for effective imagery is to be clear, confident and calm; and how to develop these qualities. Another important attitudinal issue is that most imagery exercises are done best in a state of open-minded experimentation. While most of these exercises are goal orientated and done for a specific purpose, usually with a particular outcome in mind, in an almost paradoxical way, the more open you can be and the less rigid, the more possibilities can open to you through creative imagery. This state is really one of positive expectation, which comes free of tension and with a sense of trust in the process and the beneficial outcome. This is another of the things we will discuss specifically with some of the imagery exercises that follow. It is enough here to mention it and to recommend you be aware that this open-minded, trusting attitude of experimentation can be very useful.

3. How often and when to use imagery

Some of the exercises you will be learning are recommended as one-off exercises. You do them once for a particular purpose. Others can be used almost daily. Specific recommendations will be given with each exercise.

Many imagery exercises are quite quick, taking only a few minutes. However, usually the preliminaries take a few minutes and it is often useful before you finish to spend a few minutes relaxing calmly or in meditation before you go on with your day. So, most often, ten to twenty minutes is a useful minimum time period, while some imagery exercises take longer. Again, specific recommendations will be made as we progress.

As for the ideal time of day for imagery, there are no definite rules, but you may need to experiment. Most people find morning sessions are very effective; some find themselves too sleepy at night, yet others find imagery wakes them up and hampers sleep. Others again find imagery at night works well. Ultimately, you need to experiment to find a balance with your activities and your sleep patterns.

A major principle with all meditation practices is that regular practise brings results. For many people a routine helps to maintain the discipline of the practice. Many find a morning shower followed by imagery, meditation and breakfast locks this inner work into their daily routine and helps sustain their good intentions.

Going to a like-minded and skilfully led group regularly also helps to keep your enthusiasm going, as well as providing continuing input and the benefits of good company!

4. What position to practise imagery in

Most people find they are more alert in an upright position. While you can use imagery lying down, there is the tendency to become sleepy, even if you do not completely go to sleep. Ideally, sit in a chair with an upright back or learn to sit cross-legged on the floor. An ergonomic chair can give you an excellent posture for meditation and imagery.

5. The Relaxation Response

This is the ideal technique to prepare you for any type of meditation practise. In its own right, the Relaxation Response has powerful benefits as it provides a reliable means that will help you to relax your body and calm your mind. Practising this technique regularly will alleviate stress, help you to regain and sustain that natural sense of balance, prevent illness, accelerate healing and leave you with a stronger, more enduring peace of mind.

The basics of the Relaxation Response involve learning a method of physical relaxation and then using the principles of concentration and observation to allow the physical relaxation to flow on so that your mind also becomes more relaxed and calm. In this relaxed, calm state, and being aware of all the principles we have discussed already, you will be in an open yet focused state of mind, ideally prepared for the use of the creative side of imagery.

Happily, the Relaxation Response is an easy exercise to learn and practise. For most people it is quick and satisfying and well worth regular practice. You may have learnt how to do this already but the following is a summary of what to do.

It is recommended you use this relaxation process as a preliminary to any imagery exercise, as well as taking time as a separate exercise to practise and improve your relaxation skills through learning the Relaxation Response.

For beginners, it is best to approach learning the Relaxation Response in a structured way. Then you can steadily simplify and speed up the process so eventually, while it requires little time, it can still be used as a reliable, methodical, powerful and effective preliminary to other deeper or more involved practices. This is a very old, well tested and reliable technique.

Beginning with the feet, you work up through each

muscle group of the body, contracting and relaxing the muscles. What the exercise does it is to focus your attention on each major muscle group in the body. By contracting the muscles you highlight the feeling of tension in that area. Then, relaxing the muscles, you have an exaggerated feeling of relaxation in that area. The result is the muscles are able to let go and become more deeply relaxed than they were to begin with. The effective result is a consciously relaxed body.

With each muscle group, what is required is to give your full attention to each of the following four feelings:

(a) The feeling of the muscles at rest- what the muscles feel like when you first give them your attention.

(b) The feeling of the muscles as they are contracting- what the feeling of tension is like.

(c) The feeling of the muscles as they are relaxing- the feeling of letting go. This actually is the feeling of the Relaxation Response.

(d) The feeling of the muscles when they are deeply relaxed.

The way to get the best from this exercise is to give it your full attention – to do it mindfully. To actually contract and relax each muscle group and to focus your attention on noticing the sensations that are produced as you do so. When you do this exercise and do it consciously, it is very reliable.

A good way to begin, is to read the following transcript of the exercise and then do it for yourself. If this is how you do begin, the idea is to talk yourself through it.

So read the transcript in italics, then take a few moment to become familiar with contracting and relaxing each muscle group progressively up through the body.

For the exercise itself, say the words quietly to yourself – 'contract the muscles' and 'let them go' as you actually do the exercise. Then, leaving gaps between each phrase, use the other words and phrases to evoke deeper feelings of relaxation. These other words are deliberately abstract in nature, and aim to avoid analysis or judgement. Their purpose is to help keep you focussed and to assist in the process of letting go.

Many people find it helpful to link the sayings of each phrase with their breathing. This provides a slow, steady and pleasant rhythm to it all and is inherently relaxing in its own right. To do this say ' Contracting the muscles' on an in breath, 'And let them go' on the following out breath. Then take another whole breath in and out without saying anything. Breathe in again and on the next out breath, say the next relaxing phrase like 'Letting go', 'Deeply', 'Completely' or whatever else you are using for that purpose.

Learning and practising this approach in a group is obviously helpful as you will have a direct experience of it all. A recording of this exercise can be useful if you do not have direct access to a teacher. At home, CDs are of particular benefit because they keep you on track and they help you to develop a gentle rhythm. They remind you to pay attention, they bring your focus back if you get distracted. Also, they avoid you having to think about what to do next – you can just be led by the words and flow with them. Some people, therefore, make their own

practice recordings of the exercise for the
explained already, I have made specific CDs
ment this book.

Here then is the exercise:

The Progressive Muscle Relaxation exercise (PMR) used as a prelude to meditation and imagery

You will find it best to give yourself at least 20 minutes to practise this exercise. This will leave you with some time to be still at the end, just resting with the relaxed feeling you have produced.

Go to your meditation space, take up your position, check your attitude and begin your practice.

Let your eyes close gently ... turn your thoughts inwards ... and remember that this is a time to bring the mind home ... to relax ... and let go...

Now, really concentrate on your feet ... perhaps move them a·little, really feel what they are like at the moment ... now, contract the muscles of the feet, feel the tension ... and let them go ... feel the muscles relaxing ... feel the muscles becoming soft and loose ... Feel it deeply ... completely ... more and more ... letting go ...

The calves ... contract the muscles, and let them go ... feel any tension relaxing ... soft and loose ... feel it deeply ... it is a good feeling ... a natural feeling ... feel the letting go ...

The thighs ... contract the muscles, and let them go ... feel it all through ... the legs feel warm and heavy ... soft and loose ... more and more ... letting go ...

The buttocks ... contract the muscles, and let them go ... deeply ... completely ..: feel it all through the pelvis and around

...he hips ... sometimes it helps to imagine as if a belt or band around the hips has just been loosened a little ... relaxing... releasing ... simply letting go ...

The tummy ... contract the muscles, and let them go ... feel it deeply ... calm and relaxed ... completely ... feel it all through ... more and more... letting go ...

The chest ... feel it all through the chest ... now, just allow the breath to take up whatever rhythm feels comfortable for you at the moment ... effortlessly ... effortlessly ... it is a good feeling ... feel the letting go ...

The arms ... contract the muscles, and let them go ... feel it in the hands particularly ... you might feel a warmth, a tingling flowing into the hands ... perhaps a lightness ... almost like they could be floating ... just going with it ... simply letting go ...

The shoulders ... contract the muscles, and let them go ... feel the shoulders drop a little ... feel it deeply ... more and more ... deeper and deeper ... letting go ...

The jaw ... contract the muscles, and let them go ... feel the jaw drop a little ... feel it deeply ... calm and relaxed ... the tongue soft and loose ... it is a good feeling ... feel the letting go ...

And feel it up over the nose and through the cheeks ... feel it deeply ... completely ...

Now the eyes... contract the muscles, and let them go... feel it deeply ... all through the eyes ... almost like the eyes are floating in their sockets ... the temples soft and loose ...

And feel it around the ears ... the back of the head ... up over the top of the head ... calm and relaxed ... calm and relaxed ... simply going with it ...Letting go ... simply letting go ...

Now the forehead ... contract the muscles, and let them go ... feel the forehead smoothing out ... calm and relaxed ... feel it all through ... through the body and the mind ... deeply ... Completely ... more and more ... deeper and deeper ... letting go ... effortlessly ... effortlessly ... letting go ... deeply ... completely ... letting go ... letting go ... letting go ...

Rest quietly now for a few minutes before completing the exercise, perhaps stretching a little, and then letting your eyes gently open again.

This Progressive Muscle Relaxation (PMR) exercise provides a well structured, easy to learn and reliable means of relaxing the body and calming the mind.

What is recommended next is to learn how to:

1. Simplify the PMR so you are able to relax more quickly.
2. Practise the PMR in a more thorough way so you are able to relax more deeply.
3. Combine what you have learnt from these two steps, so you can relax quickly and deeply.

Relaxing more quickly

Briefly, what comes next as you learn to relax is that you simplify the PMR in several stages. With each simplification, the aim is to end up with your body just as relaxed as you remember it having become with the practise of the full PMR; only now you get there more quickly.

First experiment with and become proficient with being able to relax each muscle group without contracting the muscles. Next, combine muscle groups so you have the sense of relaxing the legs as a whole (rather than feet, then calves, then thighs). Finally, it can be almost as if you can relax the whole body as one unit. Almost like throwing a relaxation switch! Many people find this is helped by taking a deeper breath in, then sighing the breath out, feeling almost like a wave of relaxation flowing right down through the body; releasing any tension with it and leaving you feeling calm and relaxed.

Relaxing more thoroughly

The next series of exercises involves spending more time relaxing each part of the body, so you learn to relax more thoroughly.

You can begin by choosing one big toe. Imagine as if you were travelling through that toe in your mind, feeling the skin relaxing, the tissue under the skin. Feel the muscles relaxing; travel under the nail and feel that area relaxing. Feel it too through the joints, the bones; through every part of the toe. You may even be able to imagine more minute detail, almost as if you were relaxing each cell, each atom!

Focussing your attention on the fine detail of relaxation in this way leads to a profound sense of relaxation. It releases any long-held or deep-seated tension and can be freeing in many remarkable ways. This exercise takes time and concentration, but it is highly recommended. The more you do it, the more thoroughly your body will relax, and the more familiar you will become with what it feels like to have your body deeply relaxed.

Relaxing quickly and deeply

Remembering that feeling of deep relaxation, now combine it with what you learnt of how to relax quickly. With a little more practise, soon you will be able to put the two together and relax quickly and deeply. Now you have available to you as an inner resource an ideal prelude to any meditation or imagery exercise.

However, there is one major issue to address before we explore the specific applications of imagery, and that is the question of how to deal with unpleasant, uninvited or even scary images that may occasionally present themselves.

The uninvited

While for most people the practice of imagery is beneficial and pleasant, it is not uncommon for uninvited images to come to the fore from time to time. Often these are inconsequential and can be dismissed or let go of, just like the myriad of random thoughts that tend to wander through our minds throughout the day.

However, sometimes images can form that seem to have more moment. Perhaps they have an intensity that surprises you. Perhaps they reflect issues you are worried by or perhaps they are downright scary. Sometimes too it is possible for images to form that seem quite malevolent, as if they represent some force intent on doing you harm.

The problem I have in discussing all this is I do not want to conjure up for you any negative or scary images! It is a well known fact that what you expect to happen in imagery is highly likely to occur, and I can say the appearance of negative or scary images is not a big factor in the experiences of most of the people I work with. But certainly it is common enough to warrant a forewarning, especially as the techniques to deal with all this are relatively straightforward and often lead to very important benefits in their own right.

As an interesting aside, in many Eastern cultures, where the culture is often rich with the notion of good and evil spirits, imagery can be really exciting! With different expectations, a major issue in imagery for these people is often how to deal with these more challenging images.

This is certainly an area of inner work where we need to differentiate between 'negative' and 'challenging'. In Western culture, most people instinctively label disturbing or scary images as negative. Certainly they can be very disquieting, especially if they are powerful as they sometimes are. If you plan to meditate long term, or use imagery regularly, it will be helpful to be aware that sooner or later negative images are likely to present themselves and often, paradoxically, they can be helpful. How you respond to them will be the key to your ongoing practise.

For example, Judy, the very active mother of two teenage children, also ran a busy gift shop. She began meditation, desperate to find a way of relaxing and anxious that if she did not do something soon, she would develop a stress related illness. Judy learnt from Peace of Mind and then made the effort to get up a little earlier each morning to meditate for twenty minutes. Starting with the PMR and flowing on into simple silence, Judy soon found it was working; she was coping better all round, feeling more relaxed and happier within herself.

Then, as she was meditating one day, as if from nowhere a face appeared in front of her closed eyes. It was strong and clear; the face of her much loved, but somewhat austere and feared grandfather. She was quite taken aback. He had been dead several years and the shock and surprise of this very vivid image quite upset her. Fearing the face would reappear, and being unsure what to make of it, Judy stopped meditating for many months.

Around this time, I was conducting a meditation workshop interstate, and Judy came along. During a break she tentatively asked about her experience. I explained that often these apparently scary images could be very helpful and, rather than recoiling from it, she might like to approach it in a sense of enquiry, perhaps even asking her grandfather why he was there, what he might want or what he had to offer?

In the atmosphere of the workshop, Judy felt reassured enough to let go more deeply again. Perhaps not surprisingly, her grandfather's face reappeared. This time Judy stayed with the image and asked him what he wanted. He said simply and clearly he wanted her to know he was all right and he was there to help her.

Judy told me of all this at the end of the day. Tears were in her eyes as she attempted to describe the reassurance she felt from this; reassurance her grandfather was alright and his presence was there to support her. Reassurance too, that on a grander scale, death had lost something of its sting.

Classically then, these images that come uninvited are often initially disturbing. However, far more often than not, they can be of great value when we know how to work with them.

So, what are the possibilities?

Dealing with disturbing images

There are five options available.

1. Tell the image to go away

(Some people prefer to use more emphatic and colourful language!)

This is a useful technique for minor nuisance images that tend to be a fairly regular feature of most people's inner life. A specific example would be if you were doing the Quiet Place Imagery as we did for the Inner Wisdom exercise and a snake wandered uninvited into your place of peace and calm, disturbing you and disrupting the tranquillity. You could just remind it whose head it was in anyway and tell it to go away! This works well for minor issues.

2. Open your eyes and leave the exercise

If at any stage you encounter an image you feel really uncomfortable with, you can be assured you have the option of simply opening your eyes. The image will disappear and you will be back in the room where you began! You may then prefer to get up, do something else for a while and return to your meditation or imagery when you feel more settled.

A strong word of advice here. If you have this happen, if a disturbing image does form and you get up and leave your practice, it is very important that you tell someone about it. Judy's experience recounted above is a good example of this. Keeping it to yourself tends to bottle up the fear and energy of the experience; talking about it tends to let it go. Tell a family member or confidant, or seek out a professional counsellor. Often the sharing of these experiences is accompanied by an emotional release, most commonly tears; however, there is bound to be a feeling of relief also and with that a greater capacity to integrate the experience.

If at any stage you experience recurring images that disturb you, I strongly recommend you approach a professional counsellor or therapist for help.

In my experience with the exercises throughout this book, major problems are a rare occurrence, although many people do have lesser experiences, which frequently they sort out on their own in the ways being described.

3. Choose to concentrate on a more pleasant image

As we found with the white horse and the red rose exercise, it is hard for the mind to hold two images simultaneously. Another way of dealing with 'negative' images therefore, is to use selective concentration and to focus on happier themes. There are many ways you can do it, many other things you could concentrate upon. One obvious way to do this is to recreate in your mind your Quiet Place – that place where you feel particularly peaceful and comfortable. There is more detail on this technique in the next chapter.

4. Let the image run

Rather than telling the image to go away, rejecting it or attempting to change it, you adopt the stance of curiosity and let the image develop. This becomes a bit like watching an internal video clip. Without trying to influence it, approach the image like an impartial observer, almost like someone observing an interesting movie, and notice how it proceeds. This may well lead to the disquietening nature of the image becoming more intensified, but often it leads to a transformative, positive conclusion. If you can stay with the image, sit it out as it were, this is one of the best options.

It is worth giving a powerful and dramatic example of this approach. John was a highly stressed, deeply anxious middle level executive. He had a very nervous manner, chronic skin problems, a stomach ulcer and acute shyness. He gave the impression of being permanently embarrassed in other people's company and his unease was apparent to all.

John was looking for solutions, but was so anxious and fidgety that he was one of those rare people we have met who initially really was unable to sit still to meditate.

In a personal session, John was asked to imagine a Quiet Place, a place where he could feel particularly peaceful and comfortable. John struggled to locate such a place and the torment was obvious on his face. Finally, he settled on a clearing in the middle of a large pine forest, in the dark of night, with the wind howling and the sense of an impending storm! Some quiet place! But then things seemed to rapidly deteriorate and a very dynamic imagery sequence unfolded.

One of the remarkable aspects of using imagery in a therapeutic context is that a person like John can be going through a very intense inner experience, can be completely immersed in that experience and oblivious to his surroundings, yet at the same time can speak clearly of that experience and interact with the therapist.

John said that at first he felt the forest was closing in on him. However, it seemed as if there was a narrow trail leading away from the clearing, so he headed off down this winding path. All of this was very clear in his mind. He rapidly lost all awareness of the physical surroundings his body was in; it was as if all he was describing was actually happening.

As he walked along this dark, narrow and uncertain path, there was the sense of the trees leaning over and moving in to block his way. With real fear in his voice, John described how he felt the path behind him seemed to be closing in on him in a menacing way, and he started to run. The more he ran, the more the malevolent trees closed in. He was soon moving at a frantic pace.

Finally, he managed to emerge from the forest only to find himself on the edge of a deep ravine, a wild river raging a long way down below him in the gloom. Looking to his right, John noticed a swing bridge, but as he approached it he could see it was very old. The ropes it was suspended from were worn and fragile. The wooden slats of the footbridge were decayed and many were missing. With a sense of desperation and of still being pursued, John began to clamber across, even as some of the slats collapsed under his weight and the bridge groaned and strained. Nearing the other side, the whole structure disintegrated, but he was able to leap at the last minute, catch hold of the bank and scramble up the other side.

This was all sounding like an extraordinary episode from Indiana Jones; but for John it was real, intensely real. He was sweating now, talking feverishly as he described what came next. He was confronted by a towering mountain. The only way to proceed appeared to be a narrow path that wound around its base and then headed up. The higher John went, the steeper the cliff face became. And still he had that sense of being pursued. As he was moving around the edge of the mountain, the path he was walking on became narrower and narrower. In fact, the path shrank down to become more like a ledge. John looked down from this precarious perch and described the steep drop below him, the rocks he could see at the bottom, and the turbulent river tumbling along into the darkness.

Without warning John was faced with impending doom. The ledge itself began to disintegrate – it was as if it began to merge into the rockface ahead and was closing over behind. John was left with less and less to cling to. The fear was real. John was so immersed in his imagery he felt sure he was about to fall to his death on the rocks below. The feeling of panic was very strong. Finally, there was nothing left to do. He could only let go.

As he let go, a remarkable thing happened. John had the feeling of falling a little and a sense of hopeless abandonment, but then instead of falling to his death, he began to fly! John's whole countenance changed as he said in another voice – a quiet, incredulous, happy voice – 'I'm flying, I'm flying. I can fly!' John felt himself soar like a bird, rising higher, arching gracefully, circling, delighting.

Finishing the exercise, John's face was radiant. It was clear he had been through a major experience and a huge inner transformation had taken place. He had fled his fear but it had pursued him. He had felt a huge state of panic, reached a point of desperation, abandoned all hope, let go – and then he had flown.

Given John's history, he did need ongoing support to maintain this new found freedom and confidence. But he was on the way now, and this imagery exercise had become a remarkable turning point in his life.

Some people find just following John's imagery affects them quite strongly too. We actually have used it as a therapeutic exercise for some people who have been struggling to overcome their own fear. It is certainly a dramatic, yet fairly typical, example of the benefits of allowing 'negative' images to run.

Now, be clear – you may find John's experience an interesting exercise that is quite manageable to follow. If, however, your own fears present themselves through imagery, you too may find them very scary. It does take a good deal of resolve to sit there, feel them and let them run when you are on your own. It can be done, however, and it works very well – especially if you are forewarned and know what to do.

There is still another possibility.

5. Welcome 'negative' images, communicate with them, and learn from them

Often as you meditate more, and pursue your own personal development, you come to realise it is the difficult areas that offer real gold. Often the things we experience as confronting, scary and 'negative' are things we were unable to cope with in the past or that we would have preferred to be different. Often through shame or guilt we do not want to acknowledge these things as being part of our own nature, or maybe we simply have not integrated them into our conscious awareness and life. This is the realm of the 'shadow' as it is called in Jungian psychology. It is the part of us we often choose not to face and that we attempt to contain by suppressing it in our subconscious. To do this takes ongoing energy, like keeping the lid on a pressure cooker. When we relax and meditate or use imagery, it is not surprising the pressure is released and these suppressed images can re-emerge.

Experienced meditators commonly reach a point where they welcome these images, these shadowy elements of their own underworld. They welcome them like old friends, enquire deeply into their nature, treat them with respect, compassion and humour, let them run more and more, investigate them, and then either integrate them into their conscious awareness or release them altogether.

With more advanced practice and experience, what appear to be 'negative' images often have purely passing nuisance value. We come to be able to release or move on from them in a range of easy and effective ways.

Again, with experience, you will develop an obvious sense of when one of these images is better to be dismissed or whether it warrants more attention. The images to work with are the ones that are more intense and repetitive, more demanding and often quite scary. If you can, use your will to stay with these images and open up to them, allowing the accompanying feelings to flow and let the images run. Sometimes a dialogue will be valuable. Often there will be an outcome that may be surprising, relieving, instructive and transforming.

The common experience is that when you work with these images effectively, they are truly valuable.

Having now delved into the basic theory and practice of imagery, and being forearmed with the means to experiment with more specific exercises, let us examine the areas where specific forms of imagery are most powerful and creative.

CHAPTER 8

INNER PEACE –
Imagery for relaxation, stress management and meditation

TRAVELLING INTERSTATE BY car a few years ago, I was first upon a fairly serious accident. Actually it was a really beautiful day; clear sky, not a cloud to be seen, early spring. Not a breath of wind, quite still. There had been a series of sweeping bends dropping down the side of a rather steep hillside, and towards the bottom there were two hairpin bends. Rounding the second of these very tight curves, I looked across to see a motorbike upended in the ditch; its rider lying flat out beside it. It seemed he must have lost control coming through the bend, skidded, bounced into the ditch and stopped rather suddenly.

Having delighted in motorbikes myself in earlier days, and being first on the scene, naturally I went to assist. As I made my way across the road, the deeply distressed moans of the young bike rider became more audible. And the swearing! He was lying on his back, the shirt scraped off his left shoulder, a large gouge out of the side of his helmet. But it was his left leg that was the real problem. He was leaning sideways, grasping the leg above the knee, squeezing it, obviously in great pain. My veterinary training was not necessary to see that below the knee the bone was broken clean through and markedly displaced.

The young man's face was severely distorted. His teeth were clamped firmly shut although his lips were retracted back in a grimace. His eyelids were narrowed while the eyes themselves were almost jumping out of his head, like those of a frightened animal. His forehead was deeply furrowed and as I approached there was a mixture of distress, pain, pleading and relief.

Sitting down beside him, I asked him his name. 'Steve' he groaned. Fortunately, apart from the leg, any other injuries appeared to be minor. Soon other people stopped and one called an ambulance. Steve asked me what had happened, how his leg was, and for some help to get his helmet off. There was the sense he thought the leg to be grossly mangled, so I judged it to be the right thing at the time to reassure him with the truth. I explained that the leg did have an obvious, but clean break. I gave him my opinion that it appeared to be the sort of break that would heal well and quickly. I told him help was on its way and an ambulance should be with him soon.

Then I asked Steve if he wanted some help to relax. It was all he could do to give a rather pathetic nod of his head. So I asked Steve where his favourite place in the country was. He looked puzzled; it seemed painful for him to do anything including speaking, but I asked him again – in a quiet even tone.

Steve told me there was this place down by the beach he liked to go. As it happened, this was a beach I was familiar with but I asked him to describe to me what it was like the last time he was there. What time of day had it been?

Late afternoon.

What was there to see at the beach? Steve said he liked to sit on a particular rocky outcrop and look out across the sea to a medium sized island where he knew seals lived. What was the sea like?

It was fairly calm with only a small swell running

As he described the place more, Steve started to relax a little. I suggested to him that he might like to close his eyes and imagine he was back at the place while he described it a little more to me. He seemed to sense the possibility and immediately closed his eyes. What sort of day was it?

Clear sky, light breeze, only a few clouds.

What was the beach itself like?

There is (Steve was talking in the present tense now) *a sweeping sandy beach, around a wide bay.*

What colour is the sand?

Very white, well just a hint of yellow.

And what is at the end of the beach?

It rises up to quite a high bluff.

What is on the land?

It's almost completely clear; the grass is short and mostly brown, only a few trees here and there.

So what sounds can you hear in this place Steve?

There are a few birds calling behind me. Off to the right. They sound like magpies.

What about off in the distance?

I can just hear the sound of the waves.

What about smells, can you smell anything here?

Well, there is the smell of the grass; it's a bit like it's just been cut. And there is the smell of the sea. It smells really fresh.

By now Steve's face was showing definite signs of relief. The tension was going, the distorted lines smoothing out. His breathing was slowing too, becoming a little deeper and the distress in his voice was giving way to a quieter calm.

So what temperature is it Steve? Is it warm, or cool, or neutral?

Well, it's early Spring so it is warm but there is still a bit of a bite in the air.

So what about the rocks you are on, how do they feel?

Well they are warm too, but hard.

And how does the sun feel upon your skin?

Well, it is warming; it feels good.

So what is the overall feeling for you being in this place Steve?

Well. It feels really good. It's the place I come to when I want to get away from it all, when I want time to myself. To think a bit, to just look out at the sea.

And if you were going to lie down and rest for a few moments Steve, where would be the best place to do that?

Oh, there is this grassy patch just behind the rocks. It's protected from the wind and the sun shines right down on it.

So why don't you go there now Steve, and as you do, lie down. As you lie down, feel your body relaxing, in fact feel it relaxing so much that you feel almost as if you are floating up off the ground a little. Just rest there now, feeling almost as if you are floating a few inches up off the ground.

All this conversation had taken place with Steve lying in the ditch, me sitting by his head, one hand on his head, the other on his arm. Despite quite a crowd gathering and the predictable consternation, we were able to focus on Steve's Quiet Place. The more he seemed to recreate his favourite beach in his mind, the more he seemed to relax, to be oblivious to his obvious predicament.

It was not long before the wail of the ambulance could be heard off in the distance. Steve was carefully loaded onto a stretcher and was soon speeding away with the benefit of professional care.

The experience reinforced for me the power of imagery. When the mind is focussed in this way it can provide exceptional First Aid as it disassociates from a painful, unpleasant experience and becomes absorbed in something far more pleasant. This is a great technique to use in an emergency, or at times of acute distress. As it did for Steve, it can provide rapid relief from both physical or psychological pain, help restore a degree of calm, and create a situation where whatever the real issues are, they can be addressed in a more effective way.

This then is an example of how imagery can be used to create a place of inner peace and how it can be very effective, despite starting amidst major pain and distress.

Many people find this same technique to be very helpful to use from time to time, or even regularly as a lead in to their daily meditation. Having relaxed physically, this type of 'Quiet Place Imagery' can be a useful intermediary step that helps make the transition from a busy mind to a quieter, more peaceful state. For some, this Quiet Place becomes almost like an inner sanctuary into which they can retreat to get away from the bustle and pressures of daily life.

This Quiet Place Technique can be useful in another way – as an aid in pain management. Especially for short-term pain, such as for a minor surgical or diagnostic procedure, you can close your eyes, relax a little and then imagine yourself in your Quiet Place. Some people find this works particularly well for them. It is as if they can disassociate from their body for a while by focussing their attention elsewhere and imagining that they really are in their Quiet Place. Then, once the procedure is completed, they bring their attention back to their body.

In all these contexts – first aid, meditation and pain relief – the principle that explains how the imagery works is "by association". By imagining a place you associate with feeling calm and peaceful, you immediately begin to feel more calm, more peaceful. Actually, you disassociate from the unpleasant and associate with the pleasant. You focus your mind on what you know to be pleasant.

There are a few steps to follow to develop this exercise more fully. You need to build up the details of your Quiet Place. Focus your attention as you generate and really *feel* all the sensations involved in your experience of your Quiet Place. At the same time, the more you become immersed in the feeling of this place – the more it seems as if you are really there – the better it works.

There is a preferred order to all this which focuses

attention on each of the senses in the order that comes naturally for most people.

This exercise is similar when compared to the first section of the Inner Wisdom Imagery exercise in Chapter Four, however, it is included here for completeness in a modified form to suit this specific application for inner peace.

The 'Quiet Place' exercise

Allow an image to form in your mind of a place where you feel particularly peaceful and comfortable. It may be a place that you have been to before; or it may be a fantasy place, simply allow an image to form in your mind of a place where you feel particularly peaceful and comfortable – and in a way that you can explore it in more detail.

Notice firstly where this Quiet Place is. Is it a fantasy place, or a composite of several places you know, or one specific place? Be reminded there is no right or wrong in this, just concentrate on this place, which is special for you.

Now pay attention in turn to each of the following senses, taking time to build them up as fully in your mind as you can.

1. *The visuals*: What can you see? Notice what is nearby, in the middle-ground, and off into the distance. Notice any movement. Notice too what time of day it is. If the sky is visible,

is it clear or are there clouds about? Notice the shapes and sizes of everything, e.g. if there are trees, are they short or tall, are the trunks broad or narrow? What shape are the leaves? Notice too the colours, paying close attention to the shades or variations in colour.

2. *The sounds*: What can you hear? Listen for what might be close by. What sounds are coming from further afield?

3. *The smells*: What can you smell? Notice what fragrance or odour there is in this place.

4. *The physical sensations*: What do you feel? What temperature is it? Is there any wind on your skin or sun on your face? What does it feel like? What do you have contact with? Is it hard or soft; damp or dry; warm, cool or neutral?

5. *The tastes*: What can you taste? Often in this Quiet Place Exercise taste is irrelevant, but taste may be noticeable if for example, you were in the sea and could taste the salty water.

6. *The feelings*: How does it feel to be in this place? The feelings are very important in empowering imagery, so really dwell on the good feeling that goes with your Quiet Place.

7. *Any changes*: Remember, if there is anything that would make this place even more peaceful or comfortable, then you could change it.

8. You will probably be aware of a part of this place that appeals to you most particularly. If you are not there already, go to that place so

you can rest a while. Lie down, and as you do so, feel your body relaxing completely, so much so that you feel almost as if you could float up a little off the ground. Just resting now for a few moments, floating just a few inches off the ground.

9. When you are ready you can begin to end the exercise. Be reminded that at any time you choose to in the future you can return to this exercise, and that each time you do it will be easier and even more complete.

Most people who try this exercise feel it works reasonably well. Some find it exceptionally helpful, some a non – event. About three quarters of people in my experience find it fairly easy to see their Quiet Place and to *feel* as if they are really there.

Others notice their pictures seem rather vague, indistinct or fuzzy. This need not be a problem unless it concerns you! It is that sense of being in the place, and having a strong association with the place via the feelings that seem to make it work best for most people. However, if your visual imagery is not particularly clear to begin with, most people do find it improves with practice.

There is another style of using the same principle as above on my CD: *Mind-Body Medicine*. The Healing Journey is an imagery-based exercise that leads you through a landscape and includes activities that engage you with archetypal symbols of letting go, cleansing, healing, regeneration, new beginnings, relaxation and meditation. Used regularly, this exercise can bring about sustainable changes and a heightened sense of inner peace, wellbeing and optimism

Imagery for deepening relaxation

The next useful way to consider using imagery is as a means for deepening relaxation, particularly for the letting go of long-held or deeply ingrained tension. For most people, practising the Progressive Muscle Relaxation (PMR) has the effect of relaxing the body fairly thoroughly. However, having completed the PMR, if you scan your attention through your body again, you may well find that while most of the body is reasonably well relaxed, there are some areas that still feel tense, tight or even painful. These areas will feel different from the rest of the body. Usually the feeling that goes with tension or pain is that the particular muscles involved feel harder and denser than the rest of the body; contracted or isolated. Sometimes these areas will be hotter, occasionally cooler; but almost always when you really focus your attention upon them they feel obviously tenser or more painful than the rest of the body and certainly different.

This feeling of being different to the rest of the body is a key to noticing areas that need to relax more. You can help them to relax consciously in a number of ways. Repeating the whole PMR is one way. Simply letting go more, feeling the body relaxing, that sense of the Relaxation Response flowing more, can do it for some. Imagery is another option. Two imagery techniques that work very well are the White Light Imagery exercise – see Chapter 12 and the Mindfulness for Pain Relief techniques which is detailed in *Meditation – A In-depth*

Guide. While these latter two are major healing tech-niques, they can be used just as well for physical relaxation and as a lead into meditation.

Imagery and emotional expression

Another potentially powerful way to use the principles of association and imagery for relaxation and emotional ease is by practising the techniques described by Manfred Clines in his book *Sentics.* The basic intention of this exer-cise is to spend two minutes each on a series of emotions, generating one at a time, one after the other. While Clines' book goes into some detail with all this, I have found many people benefit from using the sequence in its simple form – just allowing the feelings and images to come up as you dwell on each particular emotional state.

One of the eight states is sex which obviously is not strictly speaking an emotion like anger. However, the aim of the exercise is to generate the feeling that goes with each word. You hold the word in your mind and simply observe whatever responses develop. As feelings arise aim to be mindful of them. That is, aim to observe them without judgement, without trying to manipulate or change them. Just allow any responses to flow, but have the discipline of mind to move to the next word ever two minutes.

A useful tip is to notice where the feelings are felt in your body. In other words, take the feelings from being something you are aware of in your mind, to something that registers in your body. For example does anger tighten your stomach, grief leave an empty void in that same area? Where for you do your emotions register in

Becoming more aware of all this will give
: ease, flexibility and fluidity with your emo-
. is an area of interest, there is a large section
fulness of emotions in *Meditation — an In-depth
Guide*.

You will find that you can probably do this by just
reading the words from the book. If you choose to try
this, I suggest you do it at a time when you have some
space to yourself afterwards and preferably at a time when
you have a member of the family or a good friend around.
This is because some people find that just bringing to
mind these emotional states can have a stronger impact
than expected and it is possible to become stuck for a
while with a particular emotion. Having some support
around when you first practise this technique is therefore
highly recommended.

The intention with this exercise is to feel each emotional state for just two minutes and then to move on.

The Emotional States exercise

Go to the place where you normally practise your
meditation or imagery, or you can do this exercise
just sitting in a chair. Use the following words as
triggers, and dwell on the *feeling* that goes with
each emotional state. Build that feeling as strongly
as possible, give it two minutes, and then move to
the next.

1. No emotion

2. Anger

3. Hate

4. Grief

5. Love

6. Sex

7. Joy

8. Reverence

It can be a good idea to simply sit for a few minutes at the end of the exercise before you move off
again.

Notice how easy or difficult it was to evoke each emotion, each state of mind. What images accompanied the
feelings? How easy was it to leave each emotion and
move on to the next? Did you get stuck with any of
the emotional states? How do you feel now? Are you
still carrying one of the emotions or any of the feelings
conjured up by this exercise, or can you let them all go
and move on unaffected?

Doing this exercise regularly can build a flexibility
with emotions that can enhance the freedom of emotional expression. This can be accompanied by a calmer,
easier state of mind and more appropriate and open flow
of emotions in daily life. If you sense it to be helpful,
there is a benefit in doing the exercise daily for some
time.

There is some similarity in this exercise to that of
Inner Rehearsal – the next major area of imagery, where
we learn how to practise doing things in our mind with
the intention of improving our performance.

CHAPTER 9

INNER REHEARSAL –
The key to improved performance

BETTY WAS A keen golfer who happened to have breast cancer. She was a spritely sixty-year-old with a good deal of vigour as well as sporting grey hair and the wisdom of years. For Betty, the golf was more important than the cancer. Club competitions were the highlight of her week and she practised regularly.

In Betty's mind, her cancer was viewed as a significant but relatively minor annoyance; something she felt she could deal with. The bane of her life turned out to be her slice! Betty became an enthusiastic member of our group, where her conversations over cups of tea invariably revolved around golf – and the slice. It seemed Betty had a long history with this slice. It had become a regular part of her game since she took up golf for exercise in her early fifties. Ten years later, Betty was delighted that her general play continued to improve steadily with her years, while her frustration mounted as the slice seemed to become more deeply entrenched. Many lessons had been devoted to the slice, many hours of practise focussed on correcting this basic flaw in technique. It seemed the more she practised, the more Betty practised her slice – as a slice, it got better and better!

Salvation came in the form of a top international golfer. He joined the group to learn how to deal with his cancer, and in the wonderful way synchronicity works, he sat next to Betty. During the discussions related to imagery in the group, we were exploring the role of Inner Rehearsal – how it is possible to practise things to do with healing in your head, to practise them perfectly and condition yourself to improve the outcome.

Our golfing friend really related to all this. He explained how he spent about half his golfing practise time on the fairway and half in his armchair at home. He explained the joy of practising in your head is you can do it there perfectly! Once you learn what the ideal swing looks like, it is possible to rehearse it in your head as if you are actually doing it. He explained he was able to do some of this Inner Rehearsal as if he was in his body actually hitting the ball. He would imagine all types of shots – from the tee, fairway, rough, bunker, on the green – and practise them in his head. Sometimes he would 'watch' himself hitting the ball and he had the ability to see himself from any angle, making corrections, perfecting his technique.

The point is, swinging a golf club to hit a golf ball is an automatic action. It involves such a complex sequence of muscular activity that it is controlled by the automatic, unconscious part of the brain. We have the conscious thought, 'I will hit the ball.' But when it comes to the doing of it, the message must be relayed to that automatic part of the brain which sets it in motion.

For the action to be able to be performed, the automatic part of the brain has to learn what to do. Hitting a golf ball is not a natural, instinctual thing to do. While we may have a natural skill or aptitude, we still need to learn. It is almost as if the automatic part of the brain that controls golfing techniques needs to be programmed. This is done in part via conscious learning and input, but for most people the majority of the learning happens through the repetition of physical practice. Thus, those early lessons, the early experiences, are key events that lay the foundations for future development.

In Betty's case, her slice became programmed, encoded, very early in her golfing career. The more she practised, the more she practised her slice and the more deeply entrenched it became.

As our golfing expert continued to explain what he was doing, Betty's eyes lit up. Her whole demeanour lifted to a new level of vitality – she was excited! We talked more about the method of Inner Rehearsal after the group and Betty could not wait to get started. She figured if she did this inner work and practised a slice–free swing, she might finally rid herself of her problems. Given all the reading and lessons she had been through, she was now so familiar with what to do, she felt there was a workable solution.

Betty found the imagery came easily to her. Each morning and evening she consciously relaxed her body and went through the Relaxation Response. In the ensuing calmer, more peaceful state, with clear resolve she imagined herself following through with the perfect swing. She could see it, she could feel it. She watched the ball sailing down the middle of the fairway.

Later that year a very excited Betty returned for our Christmas celebrations. After ten years of being in the middle order, Betty had just won her club's annual competition for women! She was so delighted, it was as if the cancer was a non–event. She was so full of enthusiasm for her golf, so pleased with the demonstration of what her mind could do with the golf, that she remained fully confident of staying well and living joyfully.

Another friend who works in this field took up skiing later in life. His children had been pressing him and his wife for a few years, and the enthusiasm was sustained, so James decided to join in. Being aware of Inner Rehearsal techniques, James began his skiing during the summer – in his head! Watching videos, reading books, talking with friends who skied, James became familiar with skiing styles. Each day he relaxed, cleared his mind and then went skiing!

James did most of his Inner Rehearsal as if he was in his body actually skiing. So he imagined clear sunny days and the snow fields sloping down before him. He felt the bite of the cool winter breeze, tempered by the warmth of the sunshine and the comfort of his ski pants and jacket. He felt his hands in their thick gloves grip his stocks, he felt his feet held firm in their boots and binders. Then he imagined the freedom of skiing. He decided to rehearse parallel skiing and felt the exhilaration of the turns as he watched his progress down the slope – steady and flowing.

With winter, the sense of anticipation to head for the snow was strong. Once on the slopes, the children, who had been a trifle sceptical of Dad's inner games, struggled in the beginner's group. Meanwhile, Dad sailed off, doing in reality the smooth parallel turns his mind was now familiar with! A few lessons anchored his technique and skiing became an instant delight.

Inner Rehearsal is a mental technique nearly all elite athletes appear to use – either because they (most likely) do it naturally, or because they have learnt how to practise it. Inner Rehearsal has been demonstrated to significantly improve accuracy of free throw shooting in major league basketballers. It provides a powerful key to improving any sporting performance. It is what helped Debbie Flintoff-King to win her gold medal in the Olympics. As a technique it is easy to learn and you are bound to notice its benefits.

How to improve performance using Inner Rehearsal

1. Understand the theory

As in all imagery exercises, the more you believe in what you are doing, the better it will work. Take time to appreciate the simple links between the conscious thought (wanting to perform better), knowing what better (or best) really is, and the fact that performance is largely controlled by the automatic, unconscious part of the brain. Appreciate that by controlling the brain's automatic control centre for your sport or whatever other activity you are aiming to improve, you can program yourself for improved performance.

2. Clarify the ideal

Obviously if you are programming yourself, you need to program the best possible pattern. Talk with your coaches and your peers, read the books, watch the videos. Whenever you can, see the experts live and study how they do it. It can be helpful to imagine yourself almost in their skin, emphasising the feeling of what they are doing and how they feel themselves. Form a clear image of the ideal.

3. Relax

Use the standard preparation recommended for imagery exercises. Give yourself time and space, clarify your intention, relax physically, calm your mind – use the principles and techniques of the Relaxation Response.

4. Practise Inner Rehearsal

Imagine yourself performing in an ideal manner. This manner needs to be within the realms of possibility – for you. So imagine the best you can be and practise that. If you are a fairly short teenager, imagining yourself to be a slam dunking Michael Jordan is a good goal to work towards in the more distant future, but that may well be a separate exercise to rehearsing what you are capable of right now.

For current performance in the terms of the season you may be just starting, imagine the best performance you can for that time frame. It is fine to be a little fanciful in pushing the limit of what your best may be. Be fully optimistic! However, for this technique to work, you do need to be able to believe that your goal, your ideal is possible. Practising a performance which you feel is beyond your reach, that is impossible for you, will not work.

Remember too that this technique certainly can be used in stages. So you can imagine your performance improving to a particular level for now, do the sport or activity, experience your 'live' performance improving and then use this newly gained confidence as a base to extend your goal towards even better results.

When it comes to the actual Inner Rehearsal technique, there are various ways to go about it. You can quite safely experiment with these to find out what works best for you. In my experience, and as we have discussed already, the guiding principles are that your imagery is accurate and complete and whatever you do feels good to you.

Having said that, if it works, it probably is the ideal to practise most of your Inner Rehearsal as if you are in your body actually doing the event. Also, the more senses you can engage in the process the better. So what do you see, hear, smell, taste, touch (feel) as you do it? The more of each sense (that is relevant) you can activate and build into the imagery, the better. Also, the feeling that goes with all this is critical. The ideal is to feel calm, assured, confident, joyful, successful. Some people find it easier and more effective to watch themselves perform – almost like watching a video of themselves in action, while some almost talk themselves through the rehearsal (remember Debbie Flintoff-King). While most people find one or other of the techniques is easier for them, most benefit from practising a little of each.

5. Rest

Whenever possible, leave some time at the end of your imagery to sit quietly – either simply resting or taking a few minutes to enter into meditation. For most people, Inner Rehearsal is a straightforward technique that is both fun and rewarding to practise. May good luck and better performances be with you!

Public Speaking

Now of course this same technique can be used to improve other performances beside those in sport. Andrew was a successful Real Estate Agent whose success was built on his ability to talk with people. He was genuinely interested in what his clients wanted, was very personable and liked by many. Unfortunately for Andrew, his ease with speaking with individuals and small family or business groups did not extend to large scale public speaking.

As a result of his spectacular sales figures, Andrew was invited to speak at a National Sales Convention. While honoured, Andrew was terrified. The prospect of performing in this way filled him with dread, and his anxiety was high.

Andrew approached me thinking relaxation may be the key. I explained to him that probably this would be a good part of the solution. Once Andrew learnt to relax more thoroughly and to practise basic meditation, we had a base to work from. Then we discussed imagery.

Andrew was very confident of what to say in his speech. He had a reflective side to his nature and quite some insight. So he really had something worthwhile to offer. I reinforced this for him and reminded him that his audience would be hoping to learn something from him; that he had 'the goods' as it were, and would satisfy them well. We discussed the old trick of imagining an imposing audience as if they were all seated in front of you in their underwear! Andrew really enjoyed this imagery, the humour helping to put him at ease a little. Next we worked on Inner Rehearsal.

I instructed Andrew to begin his Inner Rehearsal practice with the Relaxation Response. Once he was feeling calm, he was to imagine the hall he would be speaking in and the audience gathered in their seats. He could imagine the atmosphere that went with the other speakers and then imagine his time was approaching. If at any point in this imagery exercise he became nervous, felt anxious or uneasy, he was to leave the imaginary speaking hall and reestablish inner peace and calm by letting go and returning to the peaceful refuge of his meditation.

This worked well for Andrew, but some I have helped actually use the Image of their Quiet Place (from the previous Chapter) as the peaceful refuge from which they foray into this type of Inner Rehearsal.

The first time Andrew attempted all this and imagined himself being introduced and walking onto the stage, his pulse raised, he felt as if he would break out in a sweat and butterflies churned in his stomach. He stayed with it as long as he could bear it, then let the image go, relaxed and re-entered the peaceful calm of his meditation. As he relaxed, he felt his tension drain away, his body relax, his breathing deepen. Staying with this calm feeling for a few minutes, he then was able to imagine walking onto the stage maintaining some degree of equanimity. This time he was able to begin his speech, running it halfway through in his mind before the fear rose up and unsettled him once more. Letting go, relaxing, back to the meditation. Settling, adjusting, integrating. With the next run through a little more progress, a growing sense of ease and confidence, the realisation it was working, that a change was possible, the start of buoyant optimism.

With a few more sessions Andrew could rehearse his speech thoroughly and comfortably in his mind. He concluded the exercise by imagining the audience applauding and friends congratulating him after the event. Next I suggested he imagine himself several weeks after the convention. Andrew was to look back on the program, feeling satisfied with his performance. Then he was to imagine the feeling of looking forward to his next opportunity to speak.

Happily, all this did work exceptionally well. Andrew admitted to being a little surprised by how much positive feedback he received and how in fact he actually did enjoy giving the talk in real life!

Treating Phobias

This same process also can work well for changing phobic patterns such as the fear of spiders. First establish a safe inner refuge where you can be filled with feelings of peace and calm. From this base, whether it be the peaceful calm of meditation or your Quiet Place, you then do as Andrew did for his speaking; you begin to imagine the thing that scares you, whether it be spiders, open spaces, flying.

Imagine whatever it is that bothers you in a way, and

at distance, that you can manage.

With spiders as the example, perhaps the best you can do to begin with is to imagine a spider locked up in a jar that is in a house some distance away! The idea is you then imagine moving progressively closer to the spider. Whenever, if ever, you feel anxiety or fear rising unmanageably, retreat to your inner sanctuary (whether it be the stillness of meditation or your Quiet Place), re-establish your peace and calm and then, once you feel the calm again, return to the imagery; return and move a little closer once more towards the image of what you used to fear. This simple imagery exercise has helped many people who were determined enough to persevere and to practise the technique regularly.

Once you have established a basic level of comfort with imagining the object of your fear and being with it in this imaginary, controlled situation, you can progress still more.

As the next step in this transformative imagery exercise, now in your mind you imagine coming across the problem suddenly, reacting quickly if needed, but calmly in whatever for you is a reasoned and comfortable manner. You may need to intersperse this more advanced practice with the reassuring calm of meditation, but with time and practice, it can free you from phobias and aversions.

This same process has been helpful for many people involved with healing. Whether it is using imagery to accelerate healing by rehearsing an ideal outcome, or learning to reprogram conditioned nausea following repeated courses of chemotherapy, there are many possibilities to detail in the Mind–Body Medicine section coming up.

As a natural extension of this Inner Rehearsal tech-nique, what we will consider next is how we can use imagery to reprogram old habits – how we can let go of old, unwanted patterns of behaviour and how we can use imagery to establish new ways of doing things.

CHAPTER 10

THE POWER OF THE MIND – I
Changing habits, realising your goals

SIMON WAS A highly successful insurance salesman who came to one of our residential lifestyle-based wellness programs. This program developed from the realisation that the success of our more specific cancer self-help programs lay in the fact that what was helping people to heal was our ability to help them to learn how to live well. The four key principles in the program – good nutrition, a positive state of mind, meditation and an effective support network – seemed to reliably transform illness into health and wellbeing. However, we soon realised that while it was wonderful to help people to overcome illness and regain health, it would be even better to prevent illness in the first place. Even more, there was the possibility to play a part in helping people to maximise their potentials and to experience a high and sustainable level of peace of mind.

So Simon joined this program to learn to meditate,

to reconsider his lifestyle in general and to take some time out for personal introspection. What surfaced quite quickly was Simon really did not like his job. Sure, he was good at it, very good. Sure, it paid his bills. Paid them well, giving him security and many choices. But no real happiness. Simon also realised he was genuinely attracted to the business world. He enjoyed being with people, working with people. Actually, he really liked the bustle of city life but became aware that with insurance work, he was working on his own most of the time. Simon decided it was time for a change.

Taking time out in a residential retreat setting provided Simon with the opportunity to reflect more deeply on his life and where he was going. Contemplating what he really wanted to do, and what he enjoyed, Simon decided human relations management met all his work criteria. Once home, Simon enrolled in a part-time Psychology degree and re-entered the world of active study. It was a major effort to maintain his family life, his competition squash and to keep his insurance work going to pay the bills. My guess is that often enough Simon would have felt the pressure and perhaps grumbled a bit with the load. However, there was never any hint of giving up, never any waver in his resolve. At the same time, Simon did not need to practise Affirmations and Imagery to do all this. There was no real effort required. His mind was made up, he was determined, he was embarking on a new career. And he did.

I imagine we can all recall episodes somewhat similar to this in our own lives. Times where we were so clear and so determined to achieve a particular goal nothing could stop us. We simply pushed on in an uncompromising way, made whatever sacrifices were necessary, did whatever it took, and fulfilled our goal. And enjoyed doing it!

Then again, I can also imagine most of us have suffered from New Year's Resolution Syndrome. You know the one – this year I am going to give up smoking! Or this year I will exercise every day! Or this year I will transform my anger. These good intentions make so much sense! They are logical choices, obviously in our best interests. Everyone around us it seems would welcome and support the changes. It should be so easy! Yet how often does it seem that only a week into January and rather than enjoying having made the changes, there is that nagging, recurrent guilt born of not only not making the change, but often enough, not even being able to remember exactly what the resolution was!

A while ago, I was talking to an old friend Margaret. She was telling me how everything in her life was going so well. Her children were all doing well at school, things seemed to be just delightful with her husband and what was really amazing her was how successful her business was. It seemed work was flooding in so fast that what had been a struggling florist shop was rapidly becoming a secure enterprise.

As we were parting, Margaret threw away an extraordinary line.

'You know Ian, it's all too good to be true!'

It's all too good to be true! Margaret was voicing her inner belief. Too good to be true! When I saw her again a few months later, her expectations had been fulfilled.

There was discord in the house, the flush of business had evaporated and she was living the struggle again.

I have another remarkable athletics story. The last of the decathlon's ten events is the 1500 metres. The other nine events revolve around speed and strength, so most decathletes struggle with the longer, endurance based 1500 metres. This was certainly the case for me. However, at the end of the best competition I ever had at the National Titles, I was approaching the bell lap, the last lap of the 1500. I was feeling terrific! I was moving easily, unexpectedly easily for me, and I felt as if I could really go on with it. Then, as the bell sounded, I heard the lap times being called. Quickly doing the mental arithmetic, I was shocked to realise I was thirty seconds ahead of my best ever time! Up until this point in my career, the way I ran the 1500m was a bit like my high jumping which was limited to "two inches over my head". I consistently ran near to my best; it was what I expected to do. But this time I was thirty seconds ahead!

Very quickly an extraordinary thing happened. Within the next fifty metres every joint in my body was aching, my muscles tired badly and soon I had slowed to a crawl. Struggling across the finish line, my time was just two seconds lower than my previous best – I had almost finished on time! In retrospect, I often wonder what would have happened if I had not heard that lap time. I suspect I would have discovered I was capable of running much faster than I had always thought I could!

It must be easy for each of us to reflect on times when goals seemed easy to achieve, other times when we seemed content (in a funny sort of way) to give up all too easily and soon. We can notice how the mind restricts us, often binds us to old patterns, and notice too those magical times when the mind sets us free.

The question is, does all this happen at random or can we have some control?. What would help us to find and sustain real happiness and to achieve our very best?

Clearly this is where our intelligence can play an active and dominant role. What the mind believes in, accepts as possible and targets, will greatly affect our lives and the lives of those around us. In this chapter, the aim is to look a little more deeply into what is happening when the mind works well, to learn the principles behind mind power and to investigate how we can train our mind to apply these principles in an intelligent and effective manner.

The specific areas we will consider are how to achieve goals in uncertain areas where our initial commitment may be faltering, how to change unwanted habits and develop more effective life patterns, and how to develop and sustain healthy emotions.

The Power of the Mind – 5 Key Principals

1. Understand the mind's natural functions and use them more efficiently.

2. Meditation supports the thinking mind.

3. Beliefs can limit us or set us free.

4. Perception is not always what it seems to be.

5. Change is possible

1. The Mind and its Natural state

The first thing to observe is that the principles and techniques we are talking about here are all based upon natural functions. We are all positive thinkers to some degree; we all achieve some of our goals, some of the time. The question simply is – does this happen often enough, effectively enough and powerfully enough to meet our needs?

Given that all these 'positive thinking' qualities, these life-affirming qualities, are basic, natural functions, and given we can all observe them working quite effortlessly in our lives some of the time, we need to consider first what would help this to happen more often. It seems when all these positive factors are flowing easily in our lives, as in Simon's story, there is a clarity, a confidence, a simple but uncompromising dedication to the goal which is quite effortless. These qualities are, in themselves, reflections of a state of mind. It is a state that seems free of doubt and uncertainty, a state that will not be put off, a state that has the clear conviction of purpose.

2. The Role of Meditation

While this clear state of mind can come to us almost as a gift in some situations, the most reliable way to develop and sustain it is through meditation. Terry is typical of the many business people I meet who start to meditate. He was telling me recently how much his confidence improved since he began to meditate regularly. As well as feeling more relaxed and calm, he said decisions just seem to be easier to make, easier to commit to, and the choices he makes seem to turn out really well for him.

Meditation then is a key to positive thinking. The more often and the more deeply you enter into the simple silence of profound meditation, the more you return to your natural state of balance. The more balanced you are, the more it seems you connect with your own inner wisdom and all it has to offer. This is another reason to recommend you maintain a regular practice of meditation.

Some say meditation is all you need. Meditate and your natural positivity will emerge. You will know what to do, make the right choices, follow through effectively. Meditate and positive emotions will flow naturally. You will be more open to love – to receiving and giving in a joyful way. Meditate and all will be well.

I would really love to be able to say it is as simple as that. To some degree it is – I emphasise to some degree! There is no doubting meditation does lead to profound benefits and it does bring out much of the best in us. For some people the positive benefits and changes meditation brings into their lives are nothing short of spectacular. It may well be that for some people meditation is enough. However, I have to say that in my experience, most people need some active work to overcome old mind patterns, old conditioning, old beliefs and old ingrained habits.

This then is where positive thinking and mind training exercises are well worth learning and practising. While there may well be other approaches that help change our old ways of thinking, our old habits, affirmations and imagery are dynamic and reliable techniques that have worked for many people.

3. Understanding the role of beliefs

As we have found in other sections of this book, when it comes to changing habits and achieving your goals through the use of affirmations and imagery, the first step ideally is to build a framework of understanding. Affirmations and imagery are techniques grounded in an intelligent understanding of how the mind works, and they utilise the remarkable creative power of the mind. As a recurring theme, the more we understand how these techniques work, the more we believe in them and the more effective they will be.

The key point is that beliefs themselves play a major role in determining our thoughts and actions. As human beings we have a fundamental commitment to act in accordance with our beliefs. We have been reminded of this by so many of the stories already told in this book. The reality is that when we are doing what we believe in, we feel comfortable, satisfied. We have peace of mind. When our actions do not match our beliefs, we feel uncomfortable, we have a deep sense something is wrong and we become highly motivated to do something about it. So what we believe in becomes a yardstick for our actions. This is because we are constantly striving to fulfil our beliefs, to live true to our beliefs.

Given this, what we do happen to believe in has a huge significance. While it would be ideal if all our beliefs did reflect a fundamental truth, it may well be the beliefs we do develop and hold onto are the reflection of a wide range of life experiences, and result in both creative and destructive expectations.

If you say 'This is too good to be true' or 'That always

happens to me' or 'That is not like me to have done...'
then you are voicing a limiting inner belief, a reflection
of your attitudes.

4. Perception and its impact on beliefs

These beliefs will be a product of either direct or second
hand experiences. Second hand in the sense that we learn
from the experiences of our parents, family, friends,
teachers; what we read or see on film. Direct experiences involve our own perception of what we take to
be real experiences. However, our perception relies upon
the five senses – what we can see, hear, taste, smell and
touch – as well as our more intuitive faculties. Scientists
often cast doubt on the validity of intuition, yet we know
our physical senses also can be quite limited in terms of
accuracy. Take sight for example. Most of us rely heavily
upon what we perceive with our sight, yet we know that
we see only a narrow band of the light spectrum. For
example, if we did have a slightly wider range of sight,
we would see with X-ray vision – and what a different
world we would live in!

What is important for us to realise is what we perceive we generally take as being real. If our perception
is inaccurate and it concerns a major life issue, we could
develop an inaccurate belief that affects our life in a major
way. Further, our perception is not only affected by the
physical senses, but our emotions and clarity of mind.
It is claimed that when angry, our capacity to perceive
and take in the truth of events happening around us is
diminished by up to 90%. We will all know of people
with befuddled minds. Minds that lack clarity for one

reason or another; maybe through the effect of drugs, old age, limited knowledge or intelligence. All these things can dramatically affect perception and the capacity to develop really useful belief systems.

Julia was a very likeable lady. Her outgoing personality had led her into a successful designing career but her personal life was dogged by emotional distress, and she had cancer. Julia spoke with frustration of how many relationships she had been in with what appeared to her to be highly suitable men. Yet time after time the relationships turned sour. Julia realised she had a huge problem; she could not allow intimacy into her life, she had barriers up to deepening relationships. She realized her relationship breakdowns had not 'just happened'. In fact more often than not she had actively destroyed them by the way she acted.

Then Julia made the connection. As a young girl she had grown up in the country amidst a large family. There seemed to have been much of the best of country life – close contact with nature, an easy lifestyle, lots of friends and time with her parents and extended family. Then at the age of seven, Julia had been diagnosed with measles. In the family's large farmhouse, the only place Julia could be isolated was in the rather large pantry. Julia went from living in the midst of a very large, open, loving family, to being confined by her parents in an internal room with no windows, poor ventilation and quite a few rats!

Julia wondered what she had done wrong. Her seven year-old-brain concluded she must have been very bad, that no-one really loved her and that she was not even worthy of love. In retrospect, now as an adult and a very mature woman, Julia knows her family really did love her, but this one powerful childhood experience over-rode all that and was anchored deep inside.

Also, as an adult, Julia was driven to succeed, and in doing so was able at least on one level to prove some self worth to herself. However, Julia came to realize her deeply held belief of being unworthy of love had sabotaged all her relationships. What she needed was to change her inner belief.

5. Change is possible – we can change our minds

Here then is the exciting truth behind all these states of mind and the habits that go with them. Beliefs such as the ones we are discussing are made up of images that are stored in the unconscious realm of our mind. As we know already, through the use of imagery we can communicate with our inner world, therefore with affirmations and imagery we have direct access to effectively changing, developing or sustaining our beliefs.

For example, Betty was a senior lady whose life had been lived helping others. She had supported her husband in his work, raised a fine family and contributed to her community. Now she had cancer with secondary spread – in medical terms, a hopeless prognosis. But Betty loved life and felt she had more to do. She came to our groups with her rather reluctant, but duty bound husband. Philip took all the sessions in, while he remained somewhat distant and aloof.

Betty's condition appeared to deteriorate at first, her pain became worse and despondency set in. Sitting in her armchair one evening, tears began to well up in her eyes.

Philip, sensing Betty's mood, asked her what was wrong. She spoke gently of how perhaps it was all too much, perhaps she should face reality, accept her fate and give up on getting well.

Now as it turned out, up until now, Betty had always been a rather negative person. She explained later that a string of events early in life had not worked out as she hoped. She had taken those experiences in and developed a pessimistic view. At a deep level, Betty had come to believe that things always went wrong for her.

Fortunately for Betty, at the groups her husband Philip had been paying attention. He had taken in the discussion of beliefs, affirmations and imagery, and he knew Betty was working on becoming more positive with the affirmation 'I am a positive person now!' Seeing his wife sitting there with gloom hanging over her head and pervading her very being, Philip said to her, 'That's strange. What are you now?' 'What do you mean?' responded Betty rather despondently. 'Oh, I thought you were a positive person now.'

Betty told me later this was a magical moment in her amazing recovery. With her husband's words, it was as if some inner switch was thrown. 'Yes' she said, 'You are right. I am a positive person now!'

From that moment on, Betty's focus was on the positive side of life. Instead of the old half empty glass she had been dealing with, now she truly saw the glass half full. She deliberately looked for the positive aspect in every situation, found it and found a wonderful inner peace. Her physical recovery was quite remarkable and over twenty years later her calm and joyful manner was a delight to all who knew her.

Here then is a summary:

How beliefs develop –
and how we can change them

1. We have a range of life experiences that we take in consciously via our five senses.

2. The perception of these experiences, the meaning and relevance we place on them, is affected by our emotional and mental state.

3. These perceptions are taken to be 'real' and are stored in the unconscious realms of the brain as memories.

4. Memories are made up of images – primarily pictures, sounds (words) and feelings. Tastes and smell can be involved to a lesser degree.

5. The emotions that accompany memories have a big bearing on how important they are to us. The more dramatic (strong) the emotions, the more prominent the memories, and the greater their impact in forming beliefs.

6. Memories accumulate to produce beliefs.

7. We have a deep-seated commitment to act in accordance with our beliefs.

8. For the purpose of these exercises, the unconscious mind cannot distinguish between a real life experience (and the set of images that go with it) and ones we generate (through the use of affirmation and imagery).

9. We can use the techniques of affirmation and imagery to establish, change or reinforce beliefs in such a way they will be effectively anchored and responded to.

The strong suggestion is to spend time reflecting on these principles. The more you understand all this, the more you contemplate and take to heart how it all works, the easier it will be to use the techniques, and the better they will work.

Once you have this solid framework of understanding, move on to the next Chapter and we will put it all into practice.

CHAPTER 11

THE POWER OF THE MIND – II
Affirmations and imagery in practice

One of the delightful things about affirmations and imagery is that they are rather simple to use. And they work! By following a fairly easy set of steps, you can develop a practice that has the potential to bring major benefits into your life. Again, the more you reinforce your practice with a good understanding, and the more clarity you have with what to do, the better it all works.

Using affirmations and imagery: the 7 key steps

1. Acknowledge where you are.

2. Set a clear goal.

3. Develop affirmations and imagery exercises to reinforce the goal.

4. Practise the affirmations and imagery.

5. Support your practice – respond to feedback.

6. Deal with any setbacks.

7. Establish your goal as a part of your ongoing life. Aim to live more fully in the moment.

1. Acknowledge where you are

This key issue relating to positive thinking was detailed in Chapter Five. If a difficulty or trauma in your life has caused you distress, fear or despair, remember you still do have the choice as to how you respond to that situation. While from the outside no-one could criticise you or blame you for becoming or feeling angry or depressed, is that what will work best for you? Are you prepared to put up with it? Do you choose to do something about it?

Often a key step in moving forward is to deeply acknowledge what seems to be a problem and to allow yourself to feel the emotions that go with the problem. Then, by expressing how you feel to a counsellor or to other people you value, you get it out of your system a little, and you are ready to move on.

However, you may also choose to re-examine, or reframe the problem into a more positive light. What can you learn from it? What in your life will change for the better as a result of this initial difficulty? How will you and those around you grow through the experience? Is it possible for you to view this problem as a challenge or an opportunity? What meaning or purpose can you find in it all?

There have been literally hundreds, (it may well be thousands) of people, who I have worked with who have reframed the obvious disaster of a cancer diagnosis in this way. Robert is a typical example. A high pow-ered-accountant involved in management takeovers and restructuring, Robert admitted to being a tough number cruncher. He hardly knew his children, fought regularly with his wife and despite material success, was deeply unhappy. His cancer diagnosis was devastating. Not only did it bring a sense of impending doom but now Robert feared the happiness he had been putting off and hoped he would get to later in life was going to elude him. He rapidly plunged into the depths of despair and strong suicidal thoughts filled his mind.

Amidst this depression Robert came to our groups and realised there was hope. He leapt at the possibilities, and with his usual flair, vigour and commitment, proceeded to turn his life around. He changed his attitude, his lifestyle, even his job. His health then changed and he became yet another to experience a medically unexplained and quite remarkable recovery.

These days, Robert thanks the cancer for what it has done for him. Like so many others, he says it was as if before his diagnosis he was living his life on automatic. He was putting up with so many compromises in his life as it was, and he was hoping that some time off in the future it would all be worthwhile and he might find hap-piness, might have time to be happy. The cancer changed all that. With the diagnosis, his future became uncertain. Realising he may not have long to live, Robert felt he had to address what was happening now. The old com-promises became unacceptable; he realised the value of relationships. He set about healing the relationship with his wife and began getting to know his children better.

He sought work where he could live his real ethics and sense of values. So much changed for the better as a result of the cancer, that Robert thanks it for helping him to reassess his priorities and putting them in order.

It is an unhappy observation that for most of us it takes a major trauma before we deeply question our priorities. So often it seems we take life for granted, put up with the compromises and hope to find happiness later. Perhaps this is one of the great gifts on offer from the many people I have worked with who have been diagnosed with cancer. Why wait? Why put it off? Life is so precious! And so uncertain. Why not take time now to re-consider what you really value and what your true priorities are?

There is a wonderful exercise you can do which provides the mechanism for working with these ideas.

This exercise, done with diligence, can give you the benefits many people get from a life threatening illness, without you having to get sick. It is highly recommended.

The 'What if?' Exercise

Give yourself time and space and sit down with pen and paper. Fantasise, imagining that for the next three months, everything in your life will stay the same. You will have all the same possibilities, all the same limitations. At the end of this time, your life (your life alone) will end. There is no bargaining, no extensions. This is a fantasy exercise and the first question is :

If you had three months to live, what would be

the ten most important things that you would do?

Take time to contemplate this question. Then write your answers down. Review them, perhaps you can rank them in order of priority.

The second part to the exercise is to consider how much of your time currently is being given to these priorities? If you are like many people, you may well find that the top priorities are getting very little time. Commonly, they are being put off. So, the second question is:

'What would it take to fulfil the priorities you have set?'

Contemplate that question.

Returning to the issue of acknowledging the problem, do all you can to develop a trust in life itself. Maybe this is as simple as determining, making the decision to trust there is meaning and purpose behind all that is happening to your life. Look for that meaning; look for the lesson, the opportunity and delve deeply into the purpose.

With that alone, many goals may well emerge.

2. Set a clear goal

Goal setting is given so much attention as it is the crucial step. With a clear goal, and a goal you can trust, and with the confidence and the commitment that comes with that clear goal, the rest follows fairly easily. Refer back to Chapter Four to re-examine the goal setting techniques already detailed.

However, when considering specific issues for personal change there is another process I have developed that has helped many people to get their goals clear. This has provided real insight into the 'New Year's Resolution Syndrome' and has helped many people to actually bring change into their lives.

It is highly recommended you take the time to do this exercise in detail. You will need a pen and some blank paper. If you use a diary or a journal, record the exercise in that.

The Personal Transformation exercise – A nine step process based upon mindfulness

1. Identify the Problem

Yes you can call it a challenge or an opportunity, but at this stage if it was not a problem you probably would not be bothering with it – so what is it? It could be an issue of physical health, a relationship issue, feelings of low self esteem, work problems, whatever is difficult in your life right now. As an example, I will use an issue from a recent group: Anne's inability to say 'no'. Briefly, Anne was what many would describe as 'a doormat'. She was shy, self effacing, unconfident and was driven to agree with whatever was asked of her. She had a charismatic, extroverted husband and she has breast cancer.

The first step is to write the heading on your paper:

1. Identify the problem

Then under the heading, write what you consider to be a problem that would benefit from resolution. In Anne's case, she wrote "inability to say no".

2. List the disadvantages of the problem

Next, identify why this issue is a difficulty for you. What is it you do not like about this problem?

Anne wrote:

- Always doing things for other people.
- No time for myself.
- Get tired.
- People expect a lot of me and keep asking more of me.
- It's hard trying to guess all the time what others want.
- I end up doing things I don't really want to do.

Make your own list, taking time to reflect, think deeply and be as thorough as possible.

The next step involves making the assumption most people are sane. If you had a problem that was one hundred percent a problem in your life, and if it had no benefits, and if you were sane, my guess is you would not put up with it. You would be doing all you could to change it. You probably would have changed it long ago.

So, if you have a problem in your life and you are effectively putting up with it at this moment, my guess is that it has to have some benefits attached

3. List the advantages of the problem

In other words, how does this problem help you? How do you benefit from it? What secondary gain might there be with this problem?

For Anne it was fairly easy to come up with quite a list. At first she wrote:

- I get lots of good feedback.
- People like me because I am so helpful.
- I feel needed, I feel as if I am being helpful and doing worthwhile things.

As Anne thought deeper, some core issues developed.

- By doing everything for everyone else, I do not have time to dwell on myself. I do not have to face myself.
- My happiness is bound up in other people's approval.
- I do not have to think what to do for myself, other people tell me what to do.
- I do not feel responsible for me; I just do what others want.

For Anne the exercise was already bringing some revelations!

4. Identify the solution

At this stage we are not concerned with how to achieve the solution, how to bring it into reality. That will come later. What we want here is an ideal solution; the best one you can believe is possible, even if you have real doubts at the moment concerning how to do it.

The question is, therefore, what would it be like if the problem was resolved and you had the ideal solution established in your life. The aim here is to begin to create an affirmation – a short, statement of an ideal, expressed in the first person, present tense, as if it were already done. So it will be, 'I am...' or ' I have...' or 'I do...' Usually, your sentence will begin with ' I am ...'

Anne needed to reflect on this for some time and discussed it with her husband Jack and our group. The main criteria for affirmations are the same as for imagery – they need to be accurate, complete and feel good.

Anne's first attempt was 'I say no'. She really struggled with this. For her, it did not feel good! From my point of view it was both negative and incomplete. Obviously there are plenty of occasions where saying 'Yes' is really the appropriate response. Anne needed something more flexible.

'I say Yes or No depending upon the circumstances,' was Anne's next attempt. Knowing her deeply ingrained pattern, it was easy to imagine her thinking most circumstances still justified saying 'Yes'; this was not the answer either.

Anne took the time to reflect more deeply on the real nature of the problem. She came to realize her core issue was a lack of self worth. In the past she had not valued herself enough to say 'No'. She had let all her boundaries down, given all her energy away and was allowing other people to live her life for her. She decided it was time to take her power back, to reaffirm her self worth and to begin living her own life once more.

Anne's next attempt to form her affirmation was 'I am worthy of love.' For Anne this meant she would love herself enough to respect her own needs. She would recognise what she could do for others and be comfortable with her limits. She would recognise when people were honouring her and her talents and asking for her for help out of that respect. To be worthy of love, Anne knew she would need to re-establish her boundaries and feel better within herself. She was optimistic with the possibility but certainly fragile. While she adopted "I am worthy of love" as her working affirmation, the next two steps highlighted her ambivalence.

5. List the advantages of the solution
This is usually easy enough and obvious enough.

Anne's list for the advantages of being worthy of love:

- I will feel good.
- I will have more control over my life.
- I will be able to say no when I need to have more time to myself.
- Relationships will probably be more genuine.

Now again, presuming we are sane, my guess is that if you had a solution that was one hundred percent advantageous, you would be so strongly drawn to it you would have taken it up long ago. If this is not the case, then it a reasonable proposition there are some disadvantages to the solution. The next step then is to enquire into what these disadvantages might be.

6. List the disadvantages of the solution
Some of these might be apparent but often you have to reflect rather deeply to get to the core issues.

For Anne, the list was very revealing:

- People might not like me if I say 'No'.
- People may think I have become selfish.
- I actually like doing things for other people.
- How will my husband react? It is worth restating here that husband Jack was a very big man, quite

charismatic and very dominant. It was easy to imagine he enjoyed having a wife who said "Yes' to all his demands, just as it was easy to imagine that for Anne it would actually be easier to go along with him and to say 'Yes'.

- It would be difficult to change; I am not sure if I could do it even if I wanted to. This brought out Anne's fear of failure – a common obstacle that limits goals people set.

You will probably be noticing what this exercise is doing is to bring our awareness more completely to the situation. It helps us to observe both sides of the problem and the solution. It is really an exercise in mindfulness and understanding. Understanding the pro's and con's means solutions and right action become more obvious and easier to follow.

7. *Choose between the problem and the solution*

This exercise tends to polarise the problem and the solution, making the choice more obvious. It becomes clear, if it was not already, that you can really only do one or the other. Faced with a problem that has both disadvantages and advantages, and a solution with advantages and disadvantages, which do you choose? Which will work better for you?

People do not always choose the solution. I remember well Jennifer, who came to a residential program where we did this exercise. She was basically well but happened to have asthma and used it as the focus for this exercise. Once she had considered how the asthma affected her and what was involved in the solution, Jennifer decided to stick with the problem! She decided to simply accept she had asthma and that was the way it was. In some ways it was a bit inconvenient, but she decided accepting it as it was, rather than struggling to change it, was the best option for now. A remarkable thing happened. Without anything changing in any other apparent way, the asthma went away! It seemed for Jennifer, with this deep recognition and acceptance (not resignation, please observe!), the underlying problem of her asthma cleared.

For Anne, however, like most people, the solution was far more appealing and she moved on to the next step. She decided to commit to developing her affirmation, "I am worthy of love."

8. How could I sabotage this goal?

This always seems a necessary step to consider, as it is what we tend to do! Besides, it is usually fun to investigate the possibilities, especially in a large group setting! Take the time to identify what might be the sort of tricks you could use to sabotage your new goal and to help you return to your old patterns. With this knowledge you will be forewarned, notice when traps are approaching and be able to offset them.

Anne expressed a delightful list.

- Put it off, say I am too busy to make the changes just yet, but I will do it later.
- Forget to do it!
- Hang out with all the most demanding people I know so it seems impossible.
- Do not tell anyone I am trying to change, so I am not too accountable.

- Do it a few times, but focus on feeling so bad about it, that I give it away.
- Worry about how my husband will react, and whether my marriage will fall apart
- Not take any risks.

Being aware of the potential hazards helps to accentuate the need to reinforce the changes.

9. How could I reinforce this goal?

This brings out all the means available for using the power of the mind and how to reinforce our good intentions. Before we consider this in detail, let me finish Anne's story.

Anne left the program all fired up for change. The mouse was ready to roar! I could not help admitting to some apprehension myself. If Anne managed to make these changes, to assert herself, and learn to say "No," how would her dominant husband Jack respond?

Several months later I met Jack again. He was so happy. He was genuinely thrilled by the changes that had taken place within Anne. He said, ' At last I have a true partner. While in many ways it was easier when she was so compliant, our relationship was very one-sided. Now we are both adjusting to more equality, and for me it is wonderful.'

In retrospect, Jack's changes were probably as amazing as Anne's. There is no doubt he created the space into which she could change, and in doing so he points to a key principle in making personal change - having good support.

With the assumption you have a clear goal identified,

let us now return to considering in more detail how to develop and reinforce your good intentions using affirmations and imagery.

3. How to develop affirmations and imagery

i) Affirmations – the three essential points:

For affirmations to be effective they must:
1. Be expressed in the first person,
2. Be expressed in the present tense,
3. Be goal orientated.

Using affirmations is a personalized process, something we do for ourself; hence, most affirmations begin with ' I am ' or 'I have,' etc.

Present time is the only time the unconscious responds to, therefore affirmations are expressed as if the goal is already achieved or reached. The aim is to give the mind a target it will lock on to and accept, hence, 'I am a positive person *now'*.

ii) Other guidelines for affirmations.

1. Be positive

Indicate what is needed, rather than what is not. The mind is goal orientated, it locks on to targets. It needs a positive direction to aim for, not something to avoid. So, rather than saying 'I am not a negative person now', as an affirmation, use 'I am a positive person now'.

2. Do not make comparisons

There is no need to say. 'I am as good as ...' or 'I am better than...' Your capacity, your potential may be to be better, or it may be to be worse. Aim to develop affirmations that encourage the development of your own full potential. Be non-judgemental of self and others.

3. Unless essential, do not specify a time for completion

As with comparisons, specifying time may slow you down or frustrate you. Part of the joy in using affirmations is that they release the power of our creativity and inner wisdom. This aspect of our being has a wonderful talent for getting us into the right place at the right time; and if we go with it, we will be content and at ease.

4. Do be specific, accurate and accountable

The mind needs a specific target. The more precise the goal and the greater its clarity, the more confident you can be of success.

5. Be realistic

You will be limited by what you believe is possible. However, it is normal to expect some internal reaction to using affirmations.

'I am a positive person now', you say. 'No, you're not,' comes that little doubting echo. That is normal. The echo is the old belief having its say. If it were not there, you would have very little need to use the affirmation in the first place.

Remember, this process directs or redirects the mind's attention and mobilises all its power and creativity. This is a process for making change, for replacing one belief with another, as well as simply establishing a new belief or goal. So do not be surprised by the echo. As long as the affirmation has more energy, more expectation, more hope, more determination and more oomph than the echo, and is repeated, it will gradually replace it and soon become the guiding force for your mind.

However, you will need to stay within the bounds of what you can believe is reasonably possible. There is no need to aim for perfection first off! Be gentle with yourself, and if necessary gradually set increasingly higher standards and goals.

7. Set ongoing goals
This follows on from what was just said. As you see yourself nearing completion of one goal, look for what comes next. Extend your planning and make new resolves.

8. Use action words and add a sense of excitement
The feeling and the emotion that goes with an affirmation has a lot to do with how quickly it will imprint and be accepted by the unconscious. Affirmations, therefore, work better when said with zest and excitement. One way to do this is to add 'Wow!' on the end of them: 'I am a positive person now – Wow!' Saying 'Wow!' encapsulates that positive, expectant feeling. If 'Wow!' does not suit you, use another word or phrase from your own vocabulary to enliven your affirmation.

Similarly, look for ways of expressing confidence, ease, a sense of being natural and joyful in all you aim for.

9. Be precise with the use of your words
Words used in affirmations are words of power. Pay great attention to how they might be interpreted. You can cover your bets by adding words like 'in an harmonious way.' Be as clear and precise as possible, consider all angles and

choose your words wisely. Meditating and contemplating on your choice of affirmations before using them is an excellent way to check their meaning and validity.

10. Keep a balance

Affirmations can have a profound effect upon your direction in life. Consider again the range of goals you are setting. Take heed of your physical, emotional, mental and spiritual needs and those of your family, friends and community. Affirmations are exciting tools to use. Aim to maintain that sense of balance.

iii) Examples for personal development

These are some favourite and well tried affirmations which can act as a guide for your own needs:

1. For health

'Every day in every way I am getting better and better.'
This is one of the oldest and most famous affirmations. It was first used over a century ago by the Frenchman, Emile Coué as detailed in his book *Self-Mastery through Conscious Autosuggestion*. This affirmation remains an extremely powerful and effective tool for mobilising our inner drive towards better health.

2. For relationships

'I greet this person with love.'

3. For self-esteem

'I am worthy of being here.'
'I am worthy of being happy.'
'I am worthy of being loved.'

Before discussing the finer details of how to combine the practical use of affirmations, imagery and feelings, let us examine how to develop imagery.

iv) How to develop imagery

While affirmations involve the intelligent use of words, imagery employs inner pictures to imprint a new goal on our subconscious mind and thus to stimulate our motivation and creativity to achieve that goal.

There are three classifications for the types of images we can use – Literal, Symbolic, and Archetypal.

1. Literal Images

With this variation, what we do is to see an image of the behaviour, event, or goal, literally. This means you visualise your goal the way you intend it to happen. Literal imagery is very practical and can be applied in any situation where there is a clear understanding of the goal.

This literal style is widely used in sport and we discussed this technique in detail in Chapter Nine.

Similarly, if you have a very tangible goal like giving up smoking, the use of literal imagery can be a great asset. Imagine yourself in situations where you used to smoke, only now you see yourself calm and relaxed, not smoking, and feeling a sense of pride and achievement. Combining this imagery with an affirmation such as, 'I am a happy, clean-mouthed non-smoker' and persevering in their use virtually assures a change in the behaviour.

While literal images are highly effective in sport and for making personal changes, they are often found wanting when you are faced with more complex situations or where your knowledge of the process required to achieve a given goal is unclear. When the goal is clear, but the mechanism for achieving it is uncertain, highly complex or to do with healing, symbolic or archetypal imagery is often far more appropriate and effective.

2. Symbolic and Archetypal Imagery

Symbols can be used as a vehicle to convey our conscious intention into the subconscious in a way that the intention can be recognized and acted upon. Take healing for example. The complexity and timing of the healing process is beyond most, if not all, conscious minds. However, one does not need sophisticated instruments to learn how to influence the body's healing functions directly. Imagery in either the symbolic or archetypal form is probably the most powerful tool for this purpose. As we have discussed before, imagery establishes a link between the conscious intention – 'I want to heal!' – and the subconscious function – which in turn directly influences how the body regulates its healing mechanisms. We will investigate how these techniques can be used for healing in the Mind–Body Medicine chapters.

4. How to practise affirmations and imagery

Affirmations are best repeated with positive expectation, with power, confidence, and good feeling. If you can do this when you first begin to use a particular affirmation, you will only need to repeat it for a minute or two a few times a day and that mind set will soon become established. When you have a more challenging belief to establish, your confidence is low, or if your mind is cluttered, you will need to practise more often and for longer periods.

The imagery that accompanies affirmations is used similarly and the time you will need to practice it will depend on the ease and clarity of using the image. While an individual session of symbolic imagery usually takes about ten minutes, archetypal imagery can be used for longer times. A session of the White Light Imagery for instance can easily occupy thirty to sixty minutes. Also archetypal imagery can be an excellent prelude to letting go into the simple silence of deeper meditation.

When we combine the use of affirmations, imagery and feelings, we establish a consciously chosen goal as an anchored belief. This belief will then act as a target which the mind will do all possible to direct us towards. This process, which is called 'imprinting', occurs easily and most effectively when there is a close connection between the conscious and the unconscious. A good example of this state is when we are in that reverie state just before going to sleep. It is when our mind is relaxed, not dwelling on anything in particular, and at peace. That state of reverie serves as an excellent time to practise affirmations and imagery.

Also, singing or joking with affirmations loosens the power of the conscious mind and its conditioned responses, and so facilitates the imprinting process. Making up jingles for your affirmations, and singing them out loud, can therefore be useful.

Looking directly into your eyes via a mirror and saying your affirmations out loud with power and conviction is extremely effective if you can do it.

Best of all is to combine imagery with your meditation. The meditation provides a poise and balance and has a stabilising effect on the whole process.

A good sequence for relaxation, imagery and meditation is:

(a) Sit in a slightly uncomfortable, symmetrical position

(b) Relax physically, inducing the relaxation response wherever possible.

(c) Begin your imagery.

You can use affirmations, imagery and feelings together. This is the most direct and effective way. Sometimes it may seem more appropriate to use either affirmations or imagery on their own, for example when an affirmation is used to change an undesired state of mind of long standing. You may well find it more effective to begin with, say, 'I am worthy of love now' as an affirmation before moving on to adding images once some confidence in the accuracy and reality of the affirmation is established. Similarly, many healing situations appear to respond well to the direct use of imagery.

(d) Let go of the imagery and rest in the natural peace and stillness of meditation before finishing the session.

5. Support your practice; respond to feedback

Reinforce your good intentions with positive thinking principles:

- Develop a support network. Discuss your goals with family and friends. Get them on side.
- Seek out allies who can support you actively. Avoid those who challenge you too directly or too strongly.

- Read books, listen to CDs, watch DVDs and attend workshops that support your goals.
- Attend a support group or meditation group relevant to your needs.
- Tell others of your goal – be accountable.
- Be prepared for setbacks. Changing habits can take time. Be prepared to persevere.
- Be gentle on yourself. Determine to be patient and reward yourself as you notice progress.
- Seek feedback. Be prepared to reassess your situation, make adjustments and move on.
- Smile regularly! Change needs to be fun to be sustained. Enjoy being alive. Change is a feature of life. If you were not changing, you would be dead. Enjoy the changes, celebrate your successes.

Enjoy!

6. Dealing with setbacks

While it may be that you move steadily and uneventfully towards your goals, it may also be that life goes up and down a little along the way. Setbacks can cause you to reassess your whole situation, strengthen your resolve and lead to useful modifications and changes.

The best insurance against disappointment is to give whatever you do your best. To do everything to one hundred percent of your ability. Then, if you have a setback, there will be no regrets, no guilt, no wondering 'What if…' or 'if only I had…'. At least you will have the comfort of knowing you have been giving it your all. There will be a level of acceptance and acknowledgment that leaves you free from looking backwards. You will be free to look forward for fresh solutions.

With this approach, answers to questions and solutions for setbacks seem to come very reliably. When I was ill, often the answers to setbacks came via books. Often when faced with another setback (there were many in my own road to recovery), it would seem as if I was drawn almost magnetically to a particular book, I would open it and there would be the answer on the page in front of me! Often too, old friends would appear unannounced and have the answers. The more I trusted in the process, whenever a question or problem presented itself, the more I expected an answer and the more rapidly it appeared. Synchronicity at work! Or is it manifestation?

7. Establish your goal – move towards the moment

While your new goal and the changes that go with it are bound to require your conscious effort to begin with, it is to be hoped that after a while it becomes effortless; a natural part of your life. As a part of this natural flow be prepared to move on from using active creative imagery techniques into the quieter stillness of meditation.

Be prepared for new qualities in your imagery and meditation.

As time goes on, your practise of imagery will develop and your quality of meditation will improve. You may discover that this leads to feeling more in tune with your life and the world around you. You will move steadily into a better experience of current time. You may well find there is then less need to practise imagery and that the process of goal setting and achievement begins to flow naturally, easily and powerfully with your passage through life.

CHAPTER 12

INVOCATION, MANIFESTATION AND IMAGERY –
Linking spirit, consciousness and matter

INVOCATION LITERALLY MEANS 'to call upon God in prayer.' This is the process wherein we think of someone or something that inspires us or represents a quality we aspire to or need more of and draw unto ourselves the presence or feeling of that person or thing.

Manifestation, to make manifest, literally means 'to make obvious to the eye or mind.' In practice, manifestation is the process whereby we turn something that begins in our mind as a thought, an idea, an intention into something that exists and is tangible in the physical world.

Many people I meet these days are struggling with the conflict they feel between the very real demands and allures of materialism, and their deeper yearning to expand their spirituality. Many, it seems, solve this conflict with busyness. By keeping busy with work, the household, entertainments, travel etc., they block out any real consideration of what life is all about, why they are here (on this planet, in this body) and where they are really going (not just tomorrow but after they die).

Paul Gauguin that great Impressionist painter said:

'Life is barely more than a fleeting moment
So little time to prepare oneself for eternity.'

Alexander the Great conquered more land and ruled over more of the world than anyone in recorded history. Yet it is said that when he died he requested he be wrapped in a simple shroud and his hands be left out for all to see. They were placed by his side, palms up, fingers outstretched. Alexander the Great wanted to demonstrate to his people what material possessions he was able to take with him!

For many people life comes with a knowing that the material world offers only fleeting delights. As a consequence, many I meet are seeking something of more substance. Many are seeking an experience of some spiritual reality, hoping for something more direct and satisfying, a way to combine their spirituality with their daily life.

Yet for many there is a cynicism to overcome, a disillusionment with the formal religion they might have grown up with, or with spiritual leaders who have abused their powers. For others there is a confusion to deal with as they struggle to integrate the suffering they see all around them with the notion of a benevolent God who appears to allow such injustices.

It seems for many people in the modern world, learnt spirituality has limited value. Reading the books, being taught dryly at school, in church or temple, may help but only to a limited degree. Knowledge acquired in this second-hand way does provide inspiration, direction and some inkling of what is available; but doubts are likely to remain. The only thing that is fully satisfying and that reliably brings a deep sense of personal assuredness and confidence is *direct experience*.

If you were able to have a direct experience of a spiritual reality, all doubts would cease and certainty would prevail. For with direct experience comes a knowing; a knowing that is unshakeable; a knowing that will sustain you throughout life and through death.

Therefore, in my opinion, of all the benefits imagery has to offer, the greatest is the very real possibility of it serving to introduce you directly to profound spiritual experience.

Imagery can act as a link between spirit, consciousness and matter.

Imagery provides a very real vehicle for activating your spiritual life, empowering this spirituality with direct experience.

In this chapter, two major practices will be introduced – invocation through the use of the White Light Imagery exercise, and the practise of 'manifestation'. In Chapter Fifteen on 'Healing the Heart' we will develop these themes further with more specific practises.

Invocation and the White Light Imagery exercise

The White Light Imagery exercise is a core practice for developing your spirituality. Also, it is a key practice for energising your system, and for healing. In essence, it is a simple practice; perhaps that is why it is so profound.

Most people find it easy to use, and it is safe and very reliable. I recommend this practice for frequent and regular use. It is particularly beneficial if you are just beginning to develop your meditation and imagery as it has such a wonderful balancing and stabilising effect.

As with simple meditation, when you practise White Light Imagery it will build a sound base that both empowers and positively focuses other inner work. With time, the practice will become clearer and more potent. I have been using this practice for over thirty years and continue to delight in the benefits I feel from it and rejoice in what it has offered to others who have learnt it. Importantly, I acknowledge the teachings and traditions of the great Tibetan Lama, Sogyal Rinpoche, who has been a wonderful teacher for me and whose book *The Tibetan Book of Living and Dying* adds greatly to what I am presenting here in a secular, straight forward manner.

There are two main forms of White Light Imagery exercise that experience has established as being most useful. You may well find one or the other particularly appealing and prefer to concentrate upon that one, or you may use either depending on the occasion.

Both these techniques use the same basic principles; however, the first technique makes a feature of using the breath. This means it requires good concentration and is a little more wilful in its practice. The second technique's approach is based on the quality of 'radiant energy' and uses a more natural sense of energy flow. This has a more passive, gentler style. Both techniques are highly effective and I recommend you experiment with both and then decide which suits you best – or it may be you alternate and use both from time to time as many people do. What follows is an outline of the common principles of the techniques, and then I will detail how to practise the two variations of the technique.

White Light Imagery – The Principles

1. As if it was in the sky above you, establish an image that represents whatever truth you hold most dear. This can be in the form of a personal embodiment such as a figure that represents God, Christ, Mother Mary, the Buddha or a favourite saint. Or you may prefer a more abstract image and use the image of radiant ball of light like a sun shining in the sky above you.

2. Focus all your attention – mind, heart and spirit – on this image and feel its presence. It needs to represent loving kindness, truth, wisdom and compassion. You need to feel it has your best interests at heart – through your body, mind and spirit. Remember you can choose to imbue your image with those qualities. While just thinking of the image of Christ, for example, may fill you with a sense of love and compassion, if you start with a more abstract ball of light, you choose to overlay it with all those life affirming qualities.

3. Make sure you imagine and consequently feel the presence of your image. This is not a casual process as if you were to you dispassionately view a picture of a saint. Here you aim to feel as if you actually are with this embodiment of goodness. It is as if Christ, the Buddha, the source of loving-kindness is actually

with you. When this is working well, you may feel a real sense of warm emotion. It is not uncommon when people first do this exercise thoroughly for them to be deeply moved by the experience.

4. Pray or wish from the depths of your being that all your negativity is cleared, released, let go of, transformed. Ask for the grace of forgiveness and feel the release that goes with accepting that as fully as possible. This may involve you in a conversation, an exchange of words with that higher power.

   It may be you use prayers you are familiar with, even if it has been some time since they were used last. The important thing is the sincerity of your intent, the focus of your concentration, and that you open to the feelings that go with the exercise.

5. Imagine this embodiment of truth you have invoked is so moved by your sincere entreaty that it responds directly. If you are relating to a figure, you will see them smile warmly, and sense their love and compassion welling up. See that energy growing in the form of light within their heart. If using the more abstract image of the sun like a ball of light, feel the response and see the light intensifying within the ball of light.

6. Next imagine a stream of this radiant light flowing down towards you – a stream of pure white radiant light – a stream of loving kindness. As this light reaches you, you either breathe it in for the first exercise, or feel it flow through you as it does in the next.

   Either way, you continue to feel the light flow into your body until every part is immersed in light.

This light has the quality and nature to purify you on every level. It transforms illness and generates radiant physical vitality. It releases destructive emotions and thoughts, purifying and cleansing you on every level. Then it fills you with life affirming energy.

7. As this sense of healing, cleansing and vitality builds, the light glows stronger. Feel now as if your body itself dissolves into the light, merging into the source and becoming one with it.

8. Rest in this blissful state of oneness as long as possible.

9. Complete the exercise consciously. When you feel it time to stop, take a few minutes to bring your awareness back to your body. It usually helps to move your feet a little, perhaps feel your hands move a little and then have a gentle stretch.

    At this point there is the need for a small caution. There are special needs for those people who do not have a good sense of their own personal boundaries or who know they have given a lot of their own power away and are trying to reclaim it. Before you finish, re-establish a sense of your own boundaries, your own personal space. What is needed is the feeling of being in your body.

    To explain – if you approach another person, there comes a point where you feel too close, as if you are entering into their space, and it gets uncomfortable (especially presuming you do not know them too well). Where that point is will be at the edges of your personal space. So some people find it worthwhile to re-establish this boundary consciously before they complete this exercise. Some people actually move their hands around their body to reinforce the effect of this practice. Obviously, you can do this as a separate imagery exercise if you find it helpful.

Sometimes too, it can be useful and pleasant to make time merely to sit quietly after this exercise, especially if it has been powerful and really touched you.

10. As you move off to engage the rest of your day, aim to take the qualities you experienced in the exercise with you. Carry the feelings of loving kindness in your heart and aim to be conscious of them throughout the day.

White Light Imagery – The Practice

When practising the White Light Imagery exercise, always begin by following the standard preliminaries recommended for imagery. Make sure you take time to consciously relax physically and calm your mind using the principles of the Relaxation Response.

When it comes to the actual practice, you may be able to read from the book, absorb the technique and then follow it through for yourself. However, this is certainly a technique which is easier to learn by being with a teacher or using a recording to guide you. You could record the exercises yourself and play them back to assist your concentration, or use the one I have produced.

The White Light Imagery exercise using breath

This is a powerful imagery sequence, which you will find rejuvenates and revitalises you. It is a wonderful way to catalyse self-healing, connect deeply with your spiritual life and to convey your love and healing wishes to others.

Once you are comfortably seated, let your eyes close gently... turn your thoughts inwards... and remember that this is a time for healing...

Feel your body relaxing... feel the muscles becoming soft and loose... feel your weight begin to settle down into your chair, your muscles relaxing... feel any tension releasing ... feel yourself relaxing deeply ... completely... more and more... deeper and deeper... letting go... feel it all through the body... feel it deeply... feel the letting go... completely... it is a good feeling... a natural feeling... feel the letting go... feel it in the forehead particularly... feel the forehead smoothing out... feel it all through... more and more... deeper and deeper... letting go... completely... deeply... letting go...

And as you feel yourself relaxing more deeply, imagine as if it is in the sky above you, whatever embodies or symbolises your own highest truth.

This may be the image of Christ, or Mother Mary; a particular Saint, the Buddha, or a figure from another tradition. Or you may have a more abstract view and imagine a ball of light like the sun which represents love, compassion, all that is life affirming and that has your own best interests at heart.

Imagine as if you are in the direct presence of this embodiment of all you value most... feel that presence and relax into it...

Maybe you choose to say something, like a prayer or a request... speaking quietly under your breath as if you are speaking to this presence...

Maybe there is a response or something is said for you, to you... listen for that.

As you feel yourself connecting more directly with this presence, become aware of your breathing... it is not important whether it be fast or slow – just become aware of your breathing... giving it your full attention... and allowing your breath to take up whatever rhythm feels comfortable for you at the moment... the breath moving in and out... quite effortlessly... effortlessly...

And as you continue to hold your attention on your breath, imagine that you are breathing in a pure white vapour that stems from the very heart, the centre of the image in the sky above you... so, with each breath in, see this pure white light moving down through your nostrils... down into your chest and filling it with a pure white light... and as you breath out, imagine that you are releasing grey light, a grey vapour, that carries with it all the old, the worn, and the unwanted... anything from which you need to be free...

As you breath in again, imagine you are breathing in the pure white light ... bringing with it all that is pure, and fresh and vital... breathing out and releasing the old, the worn and anything unwanted in your system...

breathing it out and releasing it… anything at all that you want to be free of…

Allow yourself to settle into a rhythm… breathing in the pure white light… seeing it streaming down into your chest… and breathing out the grey light… in with the white and pure.. out with the grey, the old and the worn…

And as you continue, feel the white light coming down steadily into your chest, and the strength of the light in your chest growing stronger… and brighter… and purer… displacing any old and worn and grey areas… filling your whole chest with a pure white light… a symbol of wholeness… purity… vitality… and healing… you may be feeling the light as a warmth… perhaps it even tingles a little as it flows throughout your body…

With each new breath, draw in more white light… until your chest feels like it is aglow… filled with this pure white light…, so that it feels like it is radiating pure white light… and, as you breathe in again, you feel the white light beginning to flow on… travelling down into your tummy… as you breathe out now, you can direct the white light, down into your tummy… and as you see the white light flowing down, feel it relaxing… feel it releasing… feel it healing… purifying… and feel the warm white light travelling down… relaxing… releasing… feel the warmth, the relaxation, the softness… releasing any old and worn energy… releasing any areas that are uncomfortable, painful… feel them being filled with the white light, with its comfort and ease… releasing…

relaxing... letting go...

And as you breathe in now, draw in more pure white light from its source... see it travelling down into your chest... and, as you breathe out, radiate that white light down... down through your abdomen... down into your pelvis... releasing any tension... softening... bringing warmth... relaxation... deeply... breathe in more white light and seeing it travelling down now into your legs... down your thighs... softening... releasing... filling with a new strength... purity... bringing healing... and wholeness... breathing in more white light... seeing it passing down now, into your calves... down into your feet... releasing any tension... releasing any old and worn areas.. and bringing a new vitality... bringing healing... strength... so that now your legs too are filled with this pure, bright white light...

And as you breathe in again, direct the white light across your shoulders and down your arms... feel the relaxation, the release... the softening, as your muscles loosen still more.. right down... feel the light flowing right down into your fingers... feel them soft and loose... see them filled with the pure white light... symbol of purity... a feeling of natural vitality...

As you breathe in again, draw more of the pure white light from its source... see it filling your lungs... and now see it travelling up your neck... into your head... and, as it moves upwards, feel the muscles relaxing... feel them becoming soft and loose... feeling the ease of it all... any worn areas... letting go... any diseased areas being freed, and replaced with a pure white light...

symbol of new strength... of purity... of healing... of wholeness and vitality...

So, now feel your whole body filled with this pure white light... and, with each new breath in, draw more white light from its source... and see it filling your whole body with still more white light... so that your whole body is glowing intensely with the pure white light...

And, as you breathe in more, see the white light expanding out... beyond your body... to encapsulate you, like an egg... like a cocoon of bright, pure, white light... filling you with strength and vitality... feel it as a whole... feel its unity... feel yourself to be at one with it... allow yourself to merge in the purity of the white light... feel its energy moving through you... feel yourself to be at one with it... feel yourself at peace... be still... feel it all through... deeply... completely... all through... feel yourself at one... and be still...

As you feel its sense of wholeness through you, you may now like to direct that white light to someone you care for... to share that feeling with them... and so imagine them as if they were in front of you ... and imagine, that as you breathe in... the white light passes through you and radiates like a searchlight to the person you care for... and see it fill them with its whiteness... see their body glowing white... and see them surrounded in a cocoon of pure white light... a symbol of purity... of wholeness... of healing... of renewed vitality...

And, as you breathe in... draw in more white light and radiate it to this person... feel it flowing through you... and see them filled with a new wholeness... a new sense of balance... purpose... seeing them whole and health... pure and vital... and share your experience with them... feel them filled with this same pure white light... and add your blessing...

Now bring your attention back to your own body once again... Allow yourself to merge again with the feeling of purity and wholeness of the light... breathe in... breathe in more white light... see it streaming down from the embodiment of your own truth... pouring into you like a funnel... a funnel coming down through your nose and filling your body... and this time, imagine that as you breath out, the light radiates out from your own body... spreading out around you... and flowing through the place you are in... see this white light filling the space around you... everyone nearby... filling them with purity, wholeness, health and vitality... feel your love flowing with it... feeling that warm, happy feeling going with it...

As you breath in more, draw in more of this energy... as you breathe out, radiate it beyond the space you are in... to the people around you... to the buildings around you... feel it moving off, across the country...

Breathing in more white light... drawing it down, like a funnel... drawing it down from the image above you... then through your body, and out across the land... spreading out, so that you can imagine the whole country bathed in this pure white light...

Breathing in more white light... breathing it out, and feeling it travelling right around the globe... wrapping the whole planet in a pure white light... and now share your

feeling of peace and unity with the whole planet... radi-
ate that feeling out, and feel it travelling right around,
so that the whole planet is held like a ball of pure white
light...

As you breathe in more, feel that white light streaming
down... feel yourself again merging with it... feel it
entering every part of your being... feel yourself at one
with its purity... at one with its peace... one with its
healing... feel yourself at one with its vitality... and
realise that this white light symbolises love in action...
allow yourself to merge into that feeling of love, that pure
love, streaming down and filling your whole being...
feel it all through... feel its peace... and be still... feel
yourself merging with the stillness, to allow it to be all
through you... deeply... completely... be still...

The White Light Imagery exercise using radiant energy

This version of White Light Imagery is somewhat simpler than the first. While they both have very similar elements, this one does not employ the focus on the breath, but rather concentrates on the feeling of energy flowing to you, through you and out to others. The special quality of this exercise is that you visualise the energy flowing like warm, liquid light. This is like being under a vibrant, gentle, translucent shower of warm water.

As with the first exercise, you get ready for this one just the same as if you had planned to meditate or practise any other imagery exercise.

Take up your position, relax physically.

Imagine now, as if it were in the sky above you, the highest source of power that you know. The embodiment of your own truth. It may be an image that symbolises God, or it may be the figure of Christ, Mother Mary, a particular saint or a figure from another tradition. Or you may prefer a more abstract image such as the sun which could represent the source of universal energy. Whichever of these symbolic images you find most helpful, imagine that as well as being a source of energy, this is a source of love and compassion, of loving kindness, of a presence that has your own best interest at heart.

As this image forms in your mind, allow yourself to imagine what it would feel like to come into the presence of this all-encompassing source of energy. What would it be like to feel yourself in the presence of God? Or the Buddha or Christ? Or the source of universal energy?

Sometimes as you feel yourself coming closer to that presence, you may wish to say something - a prayer, an explanation, a request... Sometimes, something may be said to you or for you... so you could listen for that.

Once you feel this presence as if it is in the sky above you... imagine that a beam of white light begins to flow from its very centre, down towards you. An outpouring of energy and loving kindness... If you are focussed upon a figure... imagine this light flowing from its very heart... If you are using the sun, imagine a shaft of light flowing from its very centre... warm, liquid, white light...

Now as this beam of warm, liquid, white light reaches

the crown of your head… it not only flows down around your body… but also it flows through your body… warm… liquid… white light… slowly flowing down through your body… almost like water filtering down through dry sand…

Warm, liquid, white light… flowing from that infinite source… and flowing down through every part of your body…. like having a wash on the inside… it washes away anything old or worn or unwanted… it brings with it a new energy… a vitality… a sense of healing and wholeness… you can feel it filling your body and your being….

You may see this quite visually or it may be more of a feeling experience… like feeling a flow of energy or a sensation of warmth moving down through your body…

When the light does flow down to the ends of your arms… it will flow out the end of the fingers… when it does reach the end of your legs… it will flow out the through the feet, washing away with it anything old, worn or unwanted…

When this light comes to difficult, tense, painful or blocked areas… it washes through them.., clearing them… relaxing them… letting them go… you may see the affected area as having a particular shape …maybe a particular colour… when the light reaches such an area… you may see that colour being washed away like a stain being washed away from clothes held under running water… you may see the area dissolving from the outside in… some people find it helpful to imagine the light being concentrated almost like a laser… this then burns

*away the affected blockage… either from the outside in or
the inside out…*

*See and feel this warm liquid light filling every part of
your body… feel the same all over… your body filled
with the vigour… the vitality… the radiance of the warm
liquid white light…*

*As this feeling becomes all encompassing… it is as if you
merge with it… almost as if you dissolve into the light…
you feel it through your body… and your mind… it is as
if you become at one with it… given that it stems from
a infinite source, this can feel like merging or reuniting
with the infinite… go with it… feel it all through… all
through…*

*You conclude by merely resting in the presence of that
light and the infinite energy it represents and carries.*

*And again, when you feel it is time to conclude, move
your feet a little, your hands and then, when you are
ready, just let your eyes open gently.*

These are both key exercises. If you were only to do one
of all the imagery exercises mentioned in this book, I
would recommend, one of these two would be the one
to start with. While White Light Imagery has so many
immediate and practical benefits, the more you do these
particular exercises and the more you enter into the spirit
of these exercises, the more it will bring your spirituality
to life.

While these exercises start by consciously invoking
a spiritual presence, manufacturing it as it were; many

people find this spiritual energy actually does come to life, that it does take on a reality that can be experienced directly. With this direct experience comes a knowing, a certainty, a sense of connectedness that is deeply satisfying. These experiences transform your life as they confirm all the finest things you may have hoped for.

Manifestation

Manifestation is the capacity to make manifest and to bring into reality the things you genuinely and reasonably need in your life. While this principle and its attendant techniques have gained much favour within the New Age movement, and have been popularised by books like *The Secret*, manifestation is based on the simple spiritual view that your needs will be met. It takes the great spiritual teachings literally. For example the classical Christian text is :

> *"Ask and it will be given to you, seek and you*
> *will find; knock and it will be opened to you.*
> *For everyone who asks receives, and he who seeks*
> *finds, and to him who knocks it will be opened'*
>
> (Luke 11, 9-10)

This theme of needs being met is expanded upon with the images of the birds and the lilies in the field being fed and clothed (Luke 12, 13-48)

In the way we are discussing it here, manifestation is to do with how we manage to find the right partner, house, therapist, job etc. It does have equal application to lesser things like meeting day to day needs such as manifesting car parking spaces! Often, in fact, the lesser issues can act as a training ground with which to experiment with the technique; to see results, to gain confidence and move on to the larger issues.

When it comes to the big issues, the key elements for manifestation are the clarity and purity of intention, backed by a deep trust in genuine needs being met. A good personal example of these principles at work comes from the time towards the end of my illness when I travelled for the first time to India to visit Sai Baba. At this pivotal moment he told me I was already healed and not to worry. His words and presence confronted me with the choice of going on as I had been, half hoping to get well; or making the leap of faith and going on with conviction. Making that leap, I also made a silent vow to myself that when I recovered I would make a return visit in gratitude.

A year later I was well, my first wife was pregnant with our first child, we were living in Queensland and broke! I arranged to lease a Veterinary practice in Adelaide and we decided that while on the move we would go via India! With virtually no money in our bank account but a strong belief in manifestation, we booked tickets, sent a cheque and hoped that in some wonderful way it would be honoured.

Rather surprisingly, the tickets arrived, we went, had an amazing series of adventures in India and returned. Years later we still wondered where the money came from! It turned out that about a year before all this had taken place I had asked my parents to raise some money for me by selling a very special painting I had bought in better times. This had taken some time and amidst all else it had slipped our minds. When the painting sold, my parents put the money into my account literally two days before the cheque for the airfare was presented. As it happened, we left for India and with all that was going on at the time, they actually forgot to tell us on our return. I feel almost obliged to reassure you that this is a true story, as between us all we did not realise the synchronicity until years later!

Some may call these often almost miraculous events coincidence. I am happy with synchronicity, but in truth it may be better described as manifestation. During my illness, these principles were so dramatically and so repeatedly demonstrated, that the reality of all this for me is beyond doubt.

After fully recovering, I returned to the Philippines and was taught the essence of manifestation as it applies to healing and life itself by a great shaman and traditional Filipino healer. Mt Terte spoke to me with a passionate fervour, teaching me these techniques literally on the night before he died.

Mr Terte also went to some lengths to caution me, as I would caution anyone contemplating using these techniques. While the principles and techniques are relatively simple and work profoundly, your motivation can markedly affect any personal cost they may have. This is where ego is the big trap. If you want something from a place of greed, desire, even aversion; if your ego is the driving motivational force behind manifestation and if, as you may well do, you succeed in manifesting what you want in this way, it is highly likely it will rebound upon you in some way. In the simplest terms this means whatever you gain from this ego-driven place will backfire on you. You will lose it, it will turn sour, it will come back to haunt you. I am hoping I am being clear enough to be a little scary and that this makes an impression. Do take this seriously.

The key step in manifestation is to separate your wants from your needs. When there is a genuine, heartfelt need that has a pure motive, then manifestation is how you can bring it into being in a conscious, joyful and effective way. Then all you need to do is give thanks for what comes. When the motivation is pure you are free to celebrate the process as well as whatever was manifested.

The Principles of Manifestation

Mr Terte was in his late seventies when he died. He had been responsible for reviving the traditional, shamanistic healing techniques of Psychic Surgery in the Philippines and had taught many, if not most of the younger healers. He had an extraordinary spiritual understanding and a huge presence. Mr Terte played a significant role in my own healing when I first visited him in 1976 and details of these events are in my biography written by Guy Allenby: *The Dragon's Blessing.*

At the time we visited the Philippines for the third time in 1979, Mr Terte developed gangrene, first in one leg and then in the other. It was an extraordinary and deeply moving experience to be present at the end of this remarkable man's life. It was necessary to pay the medical bills for this grand old man; his life having been true to his principles, he had given all his money away. Initially, he was hospitalised and we were asked to pay in advance for the amputation planned to remove his gangrenous leg. It seemed an extraordinary situation. However, before the surgery could be performed, gangrene became established in his other leg, Mr Terte refused a double amputation and he was taken to his daughter's home to die.

That evening in the half light of candles, Mr Terte, propped up on pillows and resting his head on one arm, spoke of all this. Mr Terte's English was only fair and for things like this he wanted to be clear. So he strung together quotes from the Bible, impatiently barking them out and asking his family to read the quotes. He gave the references, they were to read the passages. Humour came into it as Mr Terte grew frustrated with the time it took his daughter to find the passages. He would grab the Bible, and knowing it so thoroughly, simply open it at the right page and thrust it back to be read.

In essence, what Mr Terte said is both healing and manifestation are carried out through the action of faith, prayer and the Holy Ghost. What did he mean by that?

Faith is that level of certainty where there is no doubt, only conviction.

Prayer is the technique of clarifying needs and being able to ask confidently they will be met.

The Holy Ghost is the spirit in action. It is one way of describing the energy that provides the substance to a thought and in doing so makes it manifest in the physical world.

Obviously Mr Terte was expressing these principles in a Christian framework. He was saying that when you form a thought and you ask for it with the confidence of certainty, energy flows to convert that thought into reality.

In practical terms, we can identify the following:

The nine step process of manifestation

1. Establish a clear need.

Differentiate between needs and wants. What you set as a goal for manifestation needs to be essential, pure and necessary. Manifestation works when its motive is based upon your own necessity, on selfless service, or giving to meet another's need. Far from ego-driven, it needs to be of the heart or spirit.

2. Have a solid framework of understanding.

Understanding is vital, just as it is in all imagery work. To my mind what is needed is an understanding of the relationship between us as individuals and the ground of our being.

Ground of our being? What is that? Some may call it Universal Energy or Life Force, some may call it God. Some may call it the creative ground or the energy out of which everything arises, and into which everything dissolves when it dies or dissolves. Whatever you call it, the theory is this ground has infinite potential and we can draw upon this potential for the things we need.

You only need to believe this notion may be possible to begin working with the Laws of Manifestation. As you experiment and your experience grows, you can develop the confidence to ask and expect that your needs will be met in a wider range of circumstances. However, for this to occur you may well find you have your own set of pre-requisites. You will probably be able to reflect a little and come up with your own list. Consider forgiveness, reconciliation, spiritual commitment and practice, self worth, prayer, gratitude, and an attitude that recognises and honours the sacred in life. The sense that you have learnt from the past and it is time for change and new development. A sense of being worthy.

3. The ask.

It may well be useful to begin manifestation with prayer – whether it be formal or of your own wording. Many Christians I have helped find the following prayer useful:

'Not as I would O Lord, But as Thy will.'

There is the accompanying sense of being a small fish in a little pond who can see a small part of a big picture (pardon the well worn images but they are useful ones!)

This exercise is based in humility with the sense of doing the best you can, putting in your request and then trusting the outcome.

4. Let it go!

This is a key step that is often tricky. Let it go. It is as if you make the ask, put it out to God or the universe, and await the response. So you do not dwell on it. You do not worry or question. You wait in trust. Importantly, you do not let it go into some void or vacuum. You entrust your request to the higher power, the higher energy, and wait in expectant anticipation.

5. Act where necessary.

It may be enough to do nothing physically while you wait. There may be a lot to do. The important thing is to be clear enough within yourself to act true to yourself. Quite commonly this approach is an invitation to hard work! It is as if when you do all you can within your own sphere, the spiritual world with all its abundance is available to you and adds to your efforts. Be congruent, be authentic, be confident.

6. Avoid surprise.

When what you ask for does turn up, do all you can to avoid being surprised! After all you were expecting your needs to be met!

7. Give thanks and celebrate.

This too is a vital step. Consciously address the power you made the request to. Give thanks. Delight in what happens. Guard against boasting or pride. Practise humility. Celebrate with a sense of joy.

8. Develop trust.

With experience, this will come naturally. Not infrequently, however, needs can be met in ways that at the time seem puzzling. Often it seems it takes the benefit of hindsight to be able to reflect back and make sense of why particular things happened when they did. An obvious and dramatic example of this is the many people who come to realise major illness is almost like a gift, as it turned their lives around for the better.

Trusting this principle of needs being met – deeply trusting – is both a challenge and a freedom.

9. Accept responsibility.

In the Bible is the rejoinder:

> *'Everyone to whom much is given, of him much*
> *will be required; and of him to whom men commit*
> *much they will demand more.'*
>
> (Luke 12, 48)

Be humble, be modest, dedicate manifestation to the higher good and the good of others.

My favourite way to begin teaching the use of these principles is with car parking spaces. I find manifesting car parks incredibly reliable as long as I ask for a space at least five minutes before I get to the destination, as long as I am not surprised to find yet another park right outside where I want to go, and as long as I give thanks. You may develop your own set of rules or expectations. Give it a try, practise in other areas. Manifestation is well worth applying consciously in the more important areas of your life.

CHAPTER 13

HEALING THE BODY –
The Principles of Mind-Body Medicine

S ANDY WAS IN her late thirties, had two young children and a husband who was very successful in business. Her diagnosis of breast cancer devastated the family, particularly as the cancer had already spread into her bones. After breast surgery, her ovaries were removed in the hope this might slow down the progress of the disease.

When Sandy came to our cancer support group many years ago, she changed her diet, learnt to meditate and began to use imagery. Sandy had difficulty seeing pictures to use in imagery. She was one of those people who found 'visualisation' difficult. However, with a little experimentation and discussion, we soon found Sandy was strongly kinaesthetic – she *felt* her images. She also had a strong Christian faith. So Sandy imagined the presence of God, as if He was in the sky above her. She then prayed in a way that left her feeling connected to her God. Immersed in this feeling, she was able to feel a stream of healing energy flowing down through her head and into her body.

Sandy had seen her bone scan. She had two secondary cancers in her bones – one located in the left hip, the other one in her ribs. When she saw the scan, her attention had focussed on the lesion in her hip; she had not really taken in the one in her ribs.

About eight weeks after diagnosis, Sandy and her family were invited to make a major move to advance her husband's work. Sandy was keen to find out how her cancer was progressing, as this information may have affected their choices. Her doctors felt at best her condition may be the same; they strongly implied it was likely to be worse. They were quite unprepared for what they found! The lesion in the ribs had remained unchanged – no worse, no better. Yet the lesion in the hip was not only better, the cancer was gone and the bone had regenerated completely. It had fully healed in just eight weeks!

Sandy was delighted to share her good news with the group. But then came her realisation that she had formed a clear mental picture of the hip lesion, based upon what she had seen of her scan. With the imagery, she was able to feel this flow of energy, coming from its divine source, and as it came into her body, she felt a flow of warmth come with it. She said that for her, she knew the healing was flowing whenever she felt the warmth. Sandy realised, however, that while she had done this clearly and powerfully for the hip, she had neglected the ribs almost completely.

Obviously the next step was for Sandy to direct the

healing energy to her ribs. She went home to put this into practice but rang me a few days later very concerned. In attempting to focus on her rib, she found strong feelings rising up that in doing this she was neglecting the hip and that the cancer would recur.

Reflecting on this for a moment, I asked Sandy how big her God was? She said her God was infinite. So I asked her to consider that she was drawing healing energy from this infinite source and yet feeling there was not enough to go around. She laughed at the limitation she was imposing, and recognised the logical flaw in her feeling of inadequacy. Interestingly enough, however, it still took her about two weeks of practice before she felt fully comfortable with the notion of healing the second lesion while she adequately covered the rest of her body.

Given what was essentially good news, with one lesion completely healed, Sandy and her family decided to go ahead with their move. This involved the usual pressures of packing and unpacking, major change, readjustment, saying goodbye to friends, renewing old relationships and making new beginnings. Shortly afterwards and, conscious of the potential affects of stress, Sandy had more tests to re-assess her situation. No change – the hip all clear, the ribs still affected. Three months later, a well settled Sandy had her next tests. All clear – healed hip, healed ribs – a remarkable recovery.

Sandy's story is a dramatic example of many cases where the use of specific forms of imagery brought specific results. Coincidence? Well maybe, but there does seem to be a lot more to it.

Sarah had a similar background and problem to Sandy,

except Sarah had eleven bony secondaries that were diagnosed three years after her treatment for primary breast cancer. Sarah had seen her bone scans, fixed that image in her mind, was very visual in her imagery and relished imagining each lesion healing. She received excellent support from her family and her local GP who was actively involved with Mind-Body techniques and Integrative Medicine. Three months later, all the cancer was gone – except for one lesion in her hip. Sarah and her GP were puzzled by this until they checked with the original scan. Sarah realised she had missed seeing that particular lesion! She had retained a clear picture of all the other spots but had missed this one. Sarah adjusted her imagery. Three months later, at her next scan, the hip was clear too.

Steven's diagnosis of lung cancer led to major chest surgery with removal of the lower section of one lung in an unsuccessful attempt to rid him of the cancer. At the point where the wind pipe (bronchus) was severed to remove the lung, staples were used to seal it shut. Not long after the surgery, these staples popped open creating a broncho-pleural fistula – a large cavity filled with air in the chest. A CAT scan demonstrated that a large triangular area was affected.

Steven sought several opinions, hoping the lung might heal itself or that further surgery would fix it. His doctors were convinced the breakdown had resulted from the activity of cancer that had been left after the surgery. They told Steven the area remaining was like a buttery mass in his chest; that it could not heal itself and further surgery was dangerous and unwarranted. They offered to wait and see, and that if it did unexpectedly improve perhaps they could staple it again. Steven pressed the doctors, asking if they were sure it could not heal on its own. 'Absolutely; there is no way!' they stated emphatically.

Now Steven had some previous experience of meditation with Dr Ainslie Meares. This had helped him through a period of stress some twenty years earlier. Although he had let the practice slip, there was an experience, a foundation to build upon. And a sense of the possible. Steven returned to intensive meditation and also began a new practice – imagery. Every day, he began his meditation sessions with ten to fifteen minutes of imagery. As a bonus, Steven found that for him the imagery also provided an ideal lead into the stillness of meditation.

For his imagery, Steven brought the CAT scan to mind. In a very visual way, he saw the lesion fairly literally. Then on a microscopic level, Steven imagined filling in the hole, using symbolic bricks of a wobbly, rectangular shape that for him represented new lung cells. In his mind he envisaged these bricks slowly building up, one on top of the other, reforming healthy lung tissue and closing the gap. Three months later, a rather incredulous doctor showed Steven a healthy CAT scan with the report 'The Broncho Pleural Fistula has spontaneously healed!' Spontaneously! Steven is in no doubt that the meditation and the specific imagery work was what did it.

So how can we explain these cases, these anecdotes? Are they just coincidences? Is it just mind over matter – or is there more to it? I believe that there is a simple theoretical basis behind these and many other remarkable true stories. While it will be wonderful when these observations and hypotheses are followed up by more serious research, this theory is based upon good science, and when converted into practice through the use of imagery there is the potential to help many people overcome a wide range of illnesses.

The Rationale of Healing Imagery

To put Healing Imagery in its full context, we need to go back to basics. The body has an extraordinary ability to heal itself. It is exquisitely well designed to cope with both trauma and disease. The body's basic urge is to maintain itself in the dynamic state of balance we call health.

No doubt we have all had times where we drank too much or ate too much, and perhaps quite literally we were knocked off balance. However, the body is like a spinning top – when it is knocked off balance, its natural tendency is to do all that it can to return to that state of balance. And it does it so well!

We all know if we cut a finger, the body's reaction is to initiate a complex array of healing mechanisms that seal the cut, regenerate new tissues and restore normal function. With a broken bone, the healing mechanisms are even more complex and 'wonder-full' – that is they are full of wonder in their intricacy and their capacity to heal. No doubt too, we have all experienced some sort of infection in our lives – colds, flu, abscesses, gastric disease. Again, the body has an amazing ability to meet these challenges, overcome them and to restore the balance we equate with good health.

To understand this a little more we need to appreciate

how these healing mechanisms are controlled. In the late sixties and seventies when I went through my Veterinary training, not much was known about all this. We did know, for example, that the immune system plays a major role in the body's defences. As well as the immunity made active by our white blood cells, we knew there was cellular immunity too – that the cells of the body themselves had some capacity to resist infection and even cancer.

However, these healing mechanisms were thought to operate largely independently, and in a way removed from any central nervous system or mind control.

Current knowledge has come a long way. It is now well known the brain regulates healing in two major ways. The first by the wide variety of chemicals it produces; the other via direct nerve pathways.

What we now know is that different states of mind, different feelings and different emotions produce different and quite specific chemicals in the brain. These chemicals, called neuro-transmitters, neuropeptides or more simply, messenger molecules – are then released into the blood stream. Travelling in the blood they flow to cells of the immune system. Here they attach onto specific receptor sites on the outer membranes of those cells. This in turn triggers changes within the cells that dramatically affect their function.

This, is another key point. It is not only a matter of how many and which kinds of immune cells you have, it is a matter of how actively and effectively they are functioning. For a long time it has been known white blood cells are the front line for the immune system. Also, for a long time is has been known having too many of these cells is a problem, just as it is problematic to have too few. More recent research, however, has revealed you could have the right number and the right kinds of cells but they could still range in function from inactive, and so ineffective, to highly active and highly effective. Clearly an active, vibrant immune system made up of the appropriate number of cells is a strong prerequisite for both good health and active healing.

One of the key principles in Mind-Body medicine is that what we commonly characterise as negative thoughts readily depress immune function, while so called positive thoughts enhance it. What this means is that if you are depressed, suffer unresolved grief, or bottle your emotions, you are highly likely to release specific chemicals from your brain that will directly suppress immune function.

Happily, on the other hand, when you are inspired, feel a surge of hope or love; when you have a good laugh; other different but similarly specific messenger molecules are released from the brain, travel via the bloodstream, attach to immune cells and activate them markedly.

Furthermore, quite remarkably, it is now known that cells of the immune system, the white blood cells, produce their own messenger molecules which they in turn release back into the bloodstream. These molecules return to the brain, providing it with feedback and completing the loop of communication between the mind and the healing functions of the body. This is another key principle that helps us to understand how Mind-Body Medicine works.

What this means in effect is that there is a healing centre in the brain that has a great capacity to control and regulate healing throughout the body.

This notion of a healing centre is very similar to the fact we have a running centre in the brain. By this I mean when you decide to go for a run, the idea starts as a conscious thought in your mind. However, when it comes to the actual process of the running, that is a very complex process. Fortunately, when you go for a run you do not need to consciously think how to move this leg; and that, how to combine the movement of your legs in rhythm with your arms; how to regulate your heart rate and your breathing. That complexity is controlled by the automatic part of the brain – the running centre.

The process of going for a run begins with the conscious thought 'I will go for a run.' Then that conscious thought goes down into the unconscious, automatic part of the brain where "the running centre" picks up the message, recognises it and says 'Sure, I know how to do that; how fast do you want to go?' Again, using conscious intention, we may give the message to speed up or slow down, while the actual process of running remains under automatic direction.

Everyone it seems has needed to go to the trouble of learning how to connect the conscious desire to run with the automatic centre that actually does it for us. I love watching young children learning to walk and run. You see them struggle up onto their feet, usually hanging onto a chair or table leg. And you see the thought form: 'I'm going to walk across the room.' And off they go, full of hope, full of expectations. A few tottery steps and crash! Down they go. Yet I am still to see a toddler just lie there, give up and say 'Well I guess I am going to be one of those kids that never learns to walk!' No, it seems so natural. They get up, try again, and again, and finally master it.

It seems most of us have taken the time to learn how to connect the conscious mind with the brain's running centre. What I suggest is the same potential exists to control the healing centre; it is just that most of us have not yet learnt how to consciously connect with it.

What we need then, is a reliable mechanism that will connect the conscious intention 'I want to heal,' with that automatic, unconscious part of the brain that regulates healing. We need a link between the conscious mind and the unconscious. Sound familiar?! Obviously what can provide such a link is the creative use of imagery.

In healing, as elsewhere, imagery provides a link between the conscious intention and the automatic function.

We can use imagery as a vehicle to carry a specific message (concerning a need to heal in a specific way) from the conscious mind, through the healing centre and on directly to the body's wonderful array of healing mechanisms.

Imagery or meditation?

Before we move into the techniques that make all this possible, another important reminder of the value of meditation and balance. Remember that, in the simple silence of meditation we do return to a profound sense of balance, and in that state, healing is free to flow naturally.

So the question often arises when it comes to healing, is meditation enough or should I do imagery only? Or a bit of both?'

I encourage everyone who is engaged actively in healing to practise Mindfulness-Based Stillness Meditation. It provides that deep sense of balance, a stable foundation from which to work and within which to heal.

About three-quarters of the people affected by cancer that I help take up the practice of imagery. What I have found through this experience is that imagery is particularly helpful for people when recently diagnosed, particularly if they have their own fears and anxieties for the future, or have been given bad news badly and had their hope taken away. Also, imagery is usually easy for people who have active minds. As an added bonus it combines particularly well with any form of treatment, providing a direct means to support that treatment with the active and creative power of the mind.

The principles to have strongly in mind with the use of healing imagery are that, just as for other imagery exercises, the images need to be accurate, complete and feel good to use. This latter point is of particular importance. Often when you begin imagery, you know it could be better; you have the sense that as a beginner you are learning, but it feels good. You feel confident with where you are with it, against the background of knowing with time and more practice the actual technique will improve. This sense of feeling content and basically confident with your imagery is a vital ingredient in its successful application.

What type of imagery to use for healing

Remember too, that when it comes to technique, we can use three types of imagery – Literal, Symbolic or Archetypal. Obviously, as has been explained earlier, healing is an area involving a complex interaction of many processes that really are far better suited to being regulated by that automatic, unconscious healing centre of the brain. So literal images have very limited use, although as the examples we have already used demonstrate, semi-literal images (such as CAT scans, X-rays, and photographs of immune cells etc.) can provide a useful starting point for the imagery.

The fact is that while healing imagery is a technique that has helped many and offers great promise, it needs to be well thought through and thoroughly planned. Let us move on then to consider how we can put all this into practice.

CHAPTER 14

HEALING THE BODY – II
How to use Imagery for healing

A LMOST INVARIABLY, SYMBOLIC or archetypal imagery will work best for healing.

To begin with, here then is a summary of the necessary steps for the use of symbolic imagery.

How to use symbolic imagery for healing – the principles

1. Develop symbolic images that represent:
   (a) the illness
   (b) any treatment
   (c) the immune system and other aspects of the body's healing mechanisms.

2. Combine these images into a sequence of action in a way that removes the image of the illness and replaces it with a symbol of fully restored health.

3. Check that these symbols are accurate and complete

and that you can feel good using them.

4. Support your practice with meditation, other imagery exercises where necessary, and the general principles of positive thinking.

5. Assess your progress, modify or adapt your imagery as required. You may well find that over the longer term, the urge to practise imagery declines and you feel more fully satisfied with the ongoing practice of meditation.

Symbolic imagery for healing – the practice

1. Developing the images

The most important thing when developing your own symbolic images is that they feel good for you. They need to provide an accurate image that represents the illness for you in a way that is acceptable intellectually, and even more importantly, intuitively. There seem to be four main ways that people derive these images:

(i) By being inspired by other's images

Sometimes as you read of other people's imagery or listen to others discuss it, you are inspired and your own image springs to mind based upon what you read or hear. Having said that, in my experience it rarely works if you try to take on someone else's images just because they worked for them. As we have discussed, imagery, especially symbolic imagery, is very personal, so the best images are the ones that you come up with yourself and can identify with directly. The best measure for assessing that you have good, useful images for yourself is that they feel good and right.

An excellent example of what we are discussing here involved an elderly lady who came to me having read the Simonton's excellent book *Getting Well Again* (very useful to read if you are using healing imagery). Margaret was a small woman. Petite, well dressed, conservative and polite to a fault, she had a warm, gentle and kindly quality that was very endearing.

Margaret had taken in the Simonton's recommendation to use aggressive images. She latched on to their suggestion to imagine the cancer as being like lumps of meat in the body; the immune system as being a pack of savage, hungry dogs that were let loose to race around the body and greedily gobble up the meat (alias the cancer). As Margaret described these dogs in detail, I recoiled at the terrifying picture she presented. Asking her what she felt about these dogs, Margaret replied, "Well, actually, they scare me to death!" When I asked her how she felt about being scared to death by an image that represented her own immune system, she realised she needed to change the picture!

Talking on, it became apparent Margaret's passion in life was her garden. So, together we worked out she could imagine her body to be a beautiful garden, the cancer would be a particular form of weed and her immune system was a very wise and diligent old gardener. Margaret's chemotherapy would be a weed killer that had a very selective action. It would kill the (cancer) weeds very effectively, but the rest of the garden would be unaffected by it. Then the gardener would add compost to the garden, representing the good food that made up Margaret's new diet. With all this, the garden would thrive.

We now had an accurate image Margaret could feel good about and was consistent with her nature and life. However, to me there was a sense what she was proposing to do was still incomplete. Being a gardener myself, my experience is that once a new weed comes into the garden, you may well get rid of it, but often it comes back. Questioning Margaret on this, I found her experience matched mine. So, to offset the subtle implication in the image, and the real possibility of natural recurrence, we added to the imagery sequence. After spraying and destroying the existing weeds, Margaret's gardener was then sent on regular patrol, to seek out any new signs of weed growth and to eliminate them before they developed into any serious problem. He also was to constantly tend and support the garden, making it healthier and stronger – so healthy that illness had no part in it. With all this in place, Margaret's imagery was finally complete.

(ii) The use of semi-literal images

All the examples at the start of this chapter featured the use of semi-literal images based upon scans or X-rays. For Sandy, Sarah and Steven, what they had literally seen as a representation of their cancers (the scans and X-rays) formed the starting point for very effective imagery. However, each one of them was encouraged to regard their CAT scan or X-ray as a representation or symbol of their cancer, which of course it really is. Therefore they were using what we call semi-literal images.

It is hard to predict who will be best suited to which type of imagery, but it is easy to imagine that more literal, left-brained people may be drawn to this type of semi-literal imagery, whereas the more creative types prefer the symbols like those Margaret used. While there have been plenty of exceptions to these rules, people with a medical background often find the semi-literal approach appealing and easy to work with.

Tom was a specialist surgeon who had a rather rare and particularly nasty cancer intertwined around his spine. He was well aware of his poor medical prognosis and the fact his treatment was regarded to be purely palliative. However, Tom had a very detailed anatomical knowledge of the area affected by the cancer. He studied his X-rays and scans to form a clear picture of the extent of the cancer and the damage it had done to his spine.

He then formed a very clear picture in his mind of what the area would look like when healed again. Tom proceeded to imagine the cancer shrivelling, and the healthy tissue regenerating. He had a remarkable response to his 'palliative' treatment; the cancer disappeared and normal function of his spine returned. Tom is alive and well many years later.

We have found it often helps people with their imagery and healing when they develop a strong image of what healthy, healed tissue looks like. For example, it may sound a little weird at first, but many people with liver disease have been helped by going to the butcher and actually asking to see a healthy liver. This image can then be held in mind as the end goal.

(iii) Out of the stillness of meditation

Very often, once people have learnt the background to imagery it works well to contemplate the principles, reflect on them deeply and then wait for the images to arise spontaneously. This is a reliable process that has worked well for many people.

Henri had prostate cancer with multiple bony secondaries. He found great comfort in using the Quiet Place imagery as a lead-in to meditation. The special place he imagined was on a large flat rock, beside a river near his childhood home. As he learnt about healing imagery and was considering applying it in his own situation, a spontaneous image came to mind.

While he was meditating one day, Henri imagined sitting on his rock as he often did to relax his mind and make the transition into meditation. However, this time a spontaneous sequence arose as if he were actually doing it. He felt himself taking one of the affected bones out of his arm and in his mind he had no trouble imagining washing it in the river! Next he took a large bottle brush, pushed it up through the marrow of the bone, washing out all the cancer as he rinsed and flushed it in the river. He saw the cancer as a dark red stain that the river washed away, and he enjoyed seeing the colour trailing away downstream. Once the first bone was sparkling white and clear of cancer, he put it back and moved on to take out and clean the next. Henri went on to have a remarkable long-term recovery.

(iv) Have the body produce the image

Charles was an accountant who had led a highly stressed, if fairly successful business life. When bowel cancer was diagnosed with inoperable liver secondaries, Charles attended our residential program more out of desperation than conviction. During meditation sessions, we sometimes apply light touch in the way of Dr Ainslie Meares. This helps people to relax more directly and often helps focus their attention on particular areas. Sometimes it helps people to form an image of their illness.

Charles had been having little success with his meditation or imagery. His busy mind seemed to be ever active, that is, until he felt the gentle hands in meditation. At first he knew they belonged to one of our therapeutic team. He felt deeply reassured by the touch, deeply calmed. His thoughts settled, he could feel his state of mind changing. Then these initial hands felt as if they lifted from him, only to be replaced by two more hands. Two hands that had an even stronger quality. Charles, a long time agnostic, swears they were the hands of Christ! They filled him with a sense of unconditional love. They brought heat and energy to his liver. He began to sweat, he began to smile. He was deeply moved. He felt that healing had begun.

The feeling of the hands stayed with Charles as part of a powerful image. The whole experience transformed his attitude: he began on a healing path; he began the spiritual journey. Many years later, Charles had survived liver secondaries longer than anyone his experienced specialists know of.

For others, putting their own attention into the area of their cancer, or touching the area lightly themselves, is effective in drawing forth an image from the cancer itself.

Images derived in this way are invariably very relevant, very powerful, and when used in this way, very effective.

2. Practising the sequence of healing

This is where all the principles of imagery come into action. Most people are able to see their imagery sequence as you might watch a video or cartoon sequence. Some talk their way through the healing sequence too, either just describing to themselves what is happening, or repeating affirmations as the pictures run. Whenever possible, it is ideal to add a physical sensation to the imagery. For some this means having a sensation of a flow of energy; for others, feelings of warmth attend the healing.

Ideally, it is best to imagine the healing sequence taking place in the location of the illness itself. This means rather than imagining the healing pictures are running (literally) through your head, or on an imaginary screen in front of you, aim to focus your attention where the lesions are, feel that part of your body and superimpose the images on that place. Many people find it helpful to put their hands on or over the affected areas, so the sense of the imagery taking place at that point is strengthened.

To reiterate, the aim of the healing sequence is to start with an image of the illness, for the treatment and immune system to combine to remove the illness, and for the healthy tissue to regenerate. In the previous chapter, Steven's sequence of his lung healing was an excellent example of an image that powerfully symbolised the healthy tissue regenerating and completing the healing.

3. Checking that the images are accurate, complete and feel good

As stated frequently now, the risk with these practices

is that they may be inaccurate or incomplete, reflecting poor technique or deeper issues of doubt or self-sabotage. Very commonly the people I work with find their first attempt at Healing Imagery produces useful images that remain at the core of their practice. However, it is very common these initial images have limitations and that they can be improved upon.

The best way to check Healing Imagery is to draw your imagery sequence. All you need are some sheets of A4 paper and either coloured pencils or crayons. The aim is to draw a series of pictures, like a story board or cartoon sequence. These pictures need to start with the symbol of the disease and then demonstrate the symbolic way in which any treatment interacts with that disease, as well as the way your body's defences and healing capacities are both imagined and interact. You then finish with an image that represents you in total good health. Ideally, you do this drawing and clarification with a therapist who is experienced in the field, although a wise friend may well suffice. You explain your intention with the imagery, what the symbols mean and how they interact. Against the need for accuracy and completeness, most outsiders will pick any deficiencies.

Nancy had stomach cancer with liver secondaries. The stomach had been cleared with surgery, but the liver remained a major problem. Nancy asked me to check her imagery as she was committed to getting well and keen to pursue every possible avenue. She had seen a scan of her liver and had a clear picture of the extent of the three lesions in it. In her imagery, Nancy represented her immune system and other healing qualities with the symbol of 'Pacman.' Her Pacman had two legs and big teeth! She knew she needed the right number of them and for her this meant she needed a team of twelve! With this very personal imagery, Nancy imagined her twelve Pacmen lived in behind her liver. Three times a day she did her practice, bringing up the Pacmen (in her mind) and seeing them eat up the three cancer lesions before she put them back to rest behind liver.

This imagery was accurate enough but clearly incomplete. Nancy was directing her healing to be active three times a day for about five minutes each time (the time she was actually doing the imagery). For the rest of the day, she was metaphorically instructing her immune system to rest! Clearly Nancy needed to have her healing operating twenty-four hours a day. This is how it normally operates anyway. However, faced with this suggestion, Nancy was deeply concerned that her Pacmen would become tired and ineffective if they worked all day! After discussing this apparent dilemma, what Nancy decided she could imagine were two more teams of twelve. She set up a rotating roster, with each team working a shift while the other two rested! For Nancy this satisfactorily represented her immune system working fully and effectively. Nancy lived for many years, longer than her doctors had ever thought possible.

4. Supporting your Healing Imagery practice

Imagery becomes a vehicle for positive expectations. It puts those hopes and beliefs into practice. Therefore, your imagery practice will be supported by anything that builds your confidence, develops your belief in the possibility of healing and anything that generates conviction. So far in this book we have discussed many helpful things that have the potential to help in this regard – the benefits of simple meditation and specific positive thinking exercises with the use of affirmations and other forms of imagery. Recognise the value of an integrated approach and be reminded of the impact the company you keep can have on your state of mind.

The attitudes, hopes and beliefs of those around you can influence your own situation strongly. We have witnessed this repeatedly with young children battling cancer. Jane had an eighteen-month-old child Nathan who was not responding to his cancer treatment. His doctors told Jane and her husband Roger they were sorry, nothing seemed to be working and they did not expect Nathan to live long. Jane changed Nathan's diet onto simple wholesome food while she and Roger learnt to meditate and how to practise imagery. At least twice a day when Nathan was asleep, one or both of his parents would cradle him in their arms, enter their own state of meditation and imagine their meditative state was also encompassing Nathan. They imagined him wrapped in a warm blanket of loving, healing light that was all around and all through him. As his treatment continued, they did specific healing imagery for him, imagining the imagery projected onto his tiny body. Remarkably, his condition began to improve. To his doctor's amazement, Nathan went on to make a full recovery and is now a healthy young adult.

Partners can share meditation and imagery with the 'patient'. This needs to be done as free of ego as possible

– as free of desire and longing as possible. It is a big ask to let go of the selfish motives, and to move into a space of unconditional loving kindness, but here is an important and necessary caution. If you attempt to do this type of exercise for someone you love or care for, and find you are doing it with a sense of desperation or urgency, you may be better to leave it. You need to have a perspective that understands that in doing this exercise you are not taking on exclusive responsibility for the outcome. In other words, this exercise can help but it is only one factor. Whether your partner gets well or not will depend on many issues. What is being said here is to do your best, but do not set yourself up for mental anguish or guilt. Do the best you can, that is all you can do.

Be aware too, that the beliefs or images held by other key people around you could also have an effect. Larry Dossey in his excellent book *Healing Words* discusses the power of prayer and the impact of thought on healing. It is quite conceivable that if your doctor has a strong belief as to the outcome of your disease, those thoughts will have some impact. It is highly recommended for people with cancer who are aiming for recovery to seek out key medical people who can imagine them becoming long-term survivors. I regularly suggest patients discuss this sensitive issue with their doctors and wherever possible find a practitioner who can support them in this very important way.

5. Assess your progress, adapt as necessary

When you set yourself specific goals, it is important to assess your progress. With healing, assessments can range from easy to difficult, depending on what types of tests may be needed for useful feedback. Pain, short and long term side effects and the time involved can all be significant factors. How often to seek this feedback therefore, will depend upon how quickly it seems the condition can change and how invasive any tests may be. I am a strong advocate of backing up your feelings and intuition with a reality check in the physical world. While mind, heart and spirit have a major and profound impact on our lives, it is still a physical body we live in, so I value physical assessments and reassessment.

Quite often imagery does change with time and with healing progress. Ellie's story in Chapter One was a good example. Another concerned Tessa who had secondary spread of breast cancer into lymph nodes under her arm. She had a Pacman image (no legs, big teeth!) which represented her healing. Three times a day she reinforced the sequence of healing by imagining the Pacmen gobbling up her cancer. Then one day, as she prepared to begin the imagery, the Pacmen went on strike! They literally refused to do anything and stayed motionless.

Tessa was deeply concerned, so I recommended she go for a checkup immediately. All her cancer had disappeared. She was in remission and it appeared her Pacmen were not prepared to waste their time! They were quite happy, however, when Tessa responded to our discussion and sent her Pacmen off on patrol, roaming Tessa's body to target any loose cancer cells and to make sure no relapse could become established.

Another major issue with healing and the repeated practice of imagery is the question of whether or not the image needs to change with each session. For example Judy had breast cancer which had been treated by surgery and radiotherapy. Now she had secondaries in her liver and was using imagery to assist her healing. She had an excellent healing sequence that finished with an image of her liver being clear of cancer, returned to full health. What bothered her deeply was when she went to do her imagery at the next session (she was doing it twice each day); there was the cancer again. Sure, she could imagine getting rid of it, but by going back to the beginning each time she did her imagery practice, was she recreating it? Should it get smaller each time or should it disappear altogether after just one effective imagery exercise? Judy was confused.

This is a common problem for many people beginning healing imagery. The practical answer to it is that you are using the imagery to convey the conscious intention: 'I want to heal' directly to the healing centre, the automatic part of the brain that controls the healing process. To achieve this goal, you are rehearsing the complete sequence of healing. What the healing imagery sequence represents, therefore, is the complete process of healing from what is known of the disease at the start to the end point of complete health.

This is similar to the way we rehearse in our mind a physical journey from one place to another. We start at the beginning, imagine all the steps along the way and finish at the destination. In the case of healing, we are using the healing sequence to instruct the automatic healing centre in the brain what to do. We want it to take us from disease to health. We entrust the details of how to complete this (healing) journey to the healing centre. What we are aiming to do is to give it a very clear message of what we want – healing; so each time we rehearse the whole sequence.

Given that feedback is not so easy to obtain on the healing journey as it is when compared to a literal journey, usually we need to wait for reassessment via medical tests, which we only take from time to time. Then, based on this new evidence we may modify or adapt the imagery. Often, as Nathan and Tessa's stories indicate, the images will change spontaneously and predict or point to a change in the physical reality of the illness.

A final note on symbolic imagery in healing. Many people have found imagery to be a vital part of their healing journey. It seems fair to me to say that for many people it has played a pivotal role in catalysing remarkable healing. I have seen it happen often.

I always recommend people who use active imagery in this way to reinforce it; to balance it with the practice of simple meditation, preferably MBSM. What I then notice is that very commonly, over time – perhaps six to twelve months – people come to feel they have done enough imagery; that the meditation seems complete in itself and it is the meditation which forms the basis of their ongoing daily practise. Often as time progresses, people find imagery is something they value, enjoy to use, but only do it from time to time when the need feels ripe. Often too, the imagery they do persevere with tends to be of the more archetypal type.

So, let us conclude this section by considering archetypal imagery.

Archetypal imagery for healing

With archetypal imagery we move from personally significant symbols to more abstract and archetypal symbols. The two classical archetypal healing images are light and water. Some exercises use one or the other, some use both light and water together. The two most common forms for using these images were detailed in Chapter Twelve on Invocation – the White Light Imagery Exercise using the breath and the White Light Imagery Exercise using an energy flow.

It needs to be emphasised that these are excellent exercises for people who are healthy, as well as being powerful tools for healing. For well people, becoming familiar with White Light Imagery provides ready access to a major energy boost. When tired, you can do the exercise, draw on an infinite source of energy and rapidly revitalise your system. For example, I have used this technique often on long car trips and find it works very well for me.

For healing, the White Light Imagery exercises are the most common ones people use after coming to our programs. They are simple in their technique, combine the best of imagery principles, are relatively free of complication, work well for many and always offer the added bonus of the very real prospect of a direct and profound spiritual experience.

When used for healing, there are a few details to be aware of. An image for the illness is still required. Using a CAT scan image or X-ray for this often does link naturally with the images of water and light. Many people prefer to imagine the body in outline with the illness as a coloured lump.

This technique is highly applicable for use with cancer, multiple sclerosis and many other diseases. Once an image is formed for the disease, the light is drawn into the body with the breath, or flows in via the head, and then proceeds to remove the symbol of the illness.

White Light Healing Imagery using the breath

Using the breathing based technique, you imagine the breath as a white vapour, seeing and feeling it (perhaps with a sensation of warmth or tingling) flowing towards the illness. Usually in this context when you imagine and feel into the illness it will feel harder and denser to you than the rest of the body. A common sensation is that it has some pain associated with it. It may also feel warmer than the rest of the body (occasionally some people feel it cooler.) Usually the illness will have a colour associated with it.

As the white vapour of the breath reaches the illness, most commonly it swirls around the outside of the mass, dissolving it or perhaps causing it to burn or smoulder, releasing a grey vapour. This grey vapour, representing the residue of the illness, is then breathed out and released from the body.

White Light (vapour) accompanies the in breath, representing healing and all the life-affirming qualities coming in; grey light (vapour) flows with the out breath, representing the disease breaking down and being released. They grey out breath also carries with it anything else that is old, worn or unwanted you need to release.

Some people find it helpful to breathe in the white vapour and to direct it into the centre of the illness, imagining the illness breaking down from the inside out, rather than from the outside in (as above). As another option, it may help to focus the beam of light almost like a laser, and to imagine this concentrated shaft of light accentuating and accelerating the healing process.

White Light Healing Imagery using energy flow

Using the energy flow technique for White Light Imagery is similar in some respects except that now the light is imagined to have liquid properties as well. The liquid white light then flows down into the body and filters through it, quite slowly – a bit like water filtering down through dry sand. Again, this warm liquid white light gently but effectively washes away anything old, worn or unwanted. Often, disease can be imagined as a particular colour which can be seen to be washed away by the liquid light – a bit like a stain being rinsed from dirty clothes under a water tap. Also, the liquid white light can be directed readily to any areas that may need it more. This technique also can be done in a similar way to a laser, where a beam of liquid white light either washes or burns the disease away from the outside in, or from the inside out.

With these forms of archetypal imagery, sometimes the disease, especially when it is cancer, will be seen to be cleared completely in a particular session. Other times, and for other people, it may seem that only partial prog-ress is made. This can be fine as long as you (yourself) feel confident with the amount of progress in any given session, and you avoid any temptation or tendency to worry. Ideally, to repeat, the aim is to do these exercises with a good feeling and plenty of confidence.

Also, be aware these Healing Imagery techniques and principles apply well to pain control. As this is another large area to consider, and as it is well covered in my other books, if you are interested in this aspect, please refer to the chapters on healing meditation in Meditation – an In-depth Guide and You Can Conquer Cancer.

A final note on archetypal images. If you reflect on this for a moment, probably the most archetypal imagery of all would be to use the simple stillness of meditation. To accomplish this, you begin by asserting the belief that when you enter the stillness of meditation, your immune system will be free to heal you powerfully and effectively. Then starting with this strong conviction, by using the MBSM technique and entering the deeper stillness of meditation you will be activating subtle but powerful imagery forces. When you do this you will in fact be using the most archetypal imagery of all. It is my belief that when the two elements of archetypal imagery and the stillness of silent meditation experienced with MBSM are combined in this way, remarkable and profound healing becomes a strong possibility.

Having considered how to heal the body in some detail, now let us move on to consider how to heal the heart.

CHAPTER 15

HEALING THE HEART –
Imagery's precious gift

FORGIVENESS, EQUANIMITY, LOVE, compassion, joy. Getting to know yourself better. Making friends with yourself. Being able to give love more unconditionally. Simple warm-hearted kindness. Who could not do with more of these qualities of the heart in their life?

While we all may honour these attributes and hope to demonstrate them in our daily lives, how can we actively develop them? This is another sphere where imagery has a major contribution to make in our personal development. With imagery there are reliable techniques for fostering just these ideals. For those who are motivated, you can learn and practise imagery exercises that will help you to forgive; that will generate love, kindness and compassion.

What follows are key techniques that I have used personally and have taught to others. Some of these techniques did in fact develop out of the needs of people in our groups. Some I learnt from other teachers; most of them are taught by my own main teacher – the Tibetan Lama Sogyal Rinpoche.

For the fact is that, while over the last few centuries, the Western world has been busy developing the intellect and studying science, for thousands of years people in the East have been busy studying the mind and developing a mind science based upon wisdom. Thus, many current psychotherapy practices can be traced back to origins in Eastern techniques. Buddhist practices, particularly, are very rich in this area. You may well benefit, therefore, from referring to Sogyal Rinpoche's book, *The Tibetan Book of Living and Dying*, especially his Chapter Twelve on Compassion.

What I have done here is to put into my own words the practices I have found most beneficial. I do so, offering respect to their original sources and the many people who have helped me to be able to explain them in what I hope will be a form that is easily accessible. Having said that I would emphasise that another of Sogyal Rinpoche's many strengths is his ability to do just that – to translate ancient techniques into a form that is readily accessible for modern people, from all spiritual traditions as well as the agnostics and atheists.

While addressing 'Healing the Heart' we will focus on four main practices:

1. Getting to know our own true nature

2. Compassion

3. Forgiveness

4. The traditional and profound practice of Tonglen

These practices will be presented in a structured way. Spending some time on each and in the particular order in which they appear below will help to make each successive practice easier. Tonglen is not a beginner's practice. Any one of these techniques could be used over a long period of time, and that is what is required for most people to develop them fully.

In a practical sense, however, these techniques do interact with each other – reinforcing, supporting and making each more accessible and possible. For most it works best to focus upon each technique, working through them one at a time and spending at least a few weeks on each. You are bound to notice that some of the techniques seem to offer you more than others. The best approach is to practise each technique for long enough (usually two to four weeks) to obtain a good *feel* for it. Then you will know what you need to do – whether it is time to move on to the next technique, or to spend longer on this particular one. Here then are these key imagery practices.

1. Getting to know your own true nature

In our essence, we are whole and pure. In our essence – whole and pure. Do you know it? Do you believe it? Do you hope to experience it?

To experience this reality directly is the aim of deep spiritual practice. To experience our own true nature as being whole and pure is to know our own true worth. And it is to know from direct experience the interconnectedness of all things. It is to know that at this deep level there is a common factor, a common ground that links us all – our common and fundamental goodness.

With this knowledge of our own innate goodness and of our interconnectedness there comes a natural respect for self and for others. There comes too a capacity to recognise the sacred in all things, along with the compassion to understand the inequities and sufferings around us and a strong desire to do all we can to remedy the situation. There is a natural urge to forgive our self and others, a natural urge to be kind to our self and to others, and a natural urge to live a life based upon compassion and loving kindness.

People learn to meditate for many reasons. Stress management, increased coping skills, healing, illness, peace of mind. The greatest gift meditation offers is the possibility of a direct experience of who we really are, of our own true nature, our good heart. So learning to meditate is the greatest gift you can give your self.

And the essence of meditation is to be found in simple silence. When we let go of all our busyness, all our *doing*, and rest in our natural state of *being*, then our good heart is revealed, and we experience this essence directly.

This style of meditation, based upon simple silence, was introduced to me in 1975 at the start of my illness by the late Dr Ainslie Meares. His approach is well presented in two of his main books *Relief without Drugs* and *The Wealth Within*. In a more traditional way Sogyal Rinpoche teaches the practice of Dzogchen, the highest form of Buddhist meditation practice. This is well described in *The Tibetan Book of Living and Dying*.

My second book on meditation: *Meditation – Pure & Simple,* along with the one more recently co-authored with Paul Bedson, *Meditation – an In-depth Guide*, focuses on techniques that can help you to relax physically, calm the mind and then move into the simple stillness of profound meditation. This is the essence of the MBSM technique.

At the risk of over-repetition, I will say it again. Practising MBSM meditation provides a view and a foundation from which all else becomes more possible, more balanced and more effective. Therefore, I recommend this to be your core practice and that you spend some time each day letting go and being still. Certainly doing this will make the following practices more possible.

2. Compassion

Sogyal Rinpoche values compassion so highly that he describes it as 'the wish fulfilling jewel'. In his words, to have compassion for another person

> *"is not simply a sense of sympathy or caring for the person suffering, not simply a warmth of heart toward the person before you, or a sharp clarity of recognition of their needs and pain, it is also a sustained and practical determination to do whatever is possible and necessary to alleviate their suffering. Compassion is not true compassion unless it is active."*

Here are six wonderful imagery exercises that progressively build compassion. Prepare for each one in the standard way you would begin any practice. Attend to your outer environment, your attitude and then relax physically and calm your mind through the use of the

Relaxation Response. Then you are ready to begin. Most people find these exercises easier with their eyes closed.

(a) The Loving Kindness exercise

Imagine, as if they were in front of you,
the person who has loved you most in life.
Traditionally your mother is recommended, but if
that is not so easy, recall a person and a time when
you felt deeply loved. Most importantly recall
the feeling, this person's unconditional positive
regard for you (their love), their acceptance, their
warmth. Give yourself over to those feelings; the
aim is to build the feeling of loving kindness as
strongly and clearly as you can. As you feel that
love rising within your heart, return the loving
feeling to this precious person. Return the love as
if you are radiating it back to them.

Now imagine a neutral person in your life as if
they were on the right of the person who loved
you most. This will be a person who you know
quite casually, but who you know well enough
to bring to mind clearly. As you imagine them
in front of you, radiate those feelings of loving
kindness to them. You may do this simply in a
feeling sense, radiating the feeling to them and
feeling it wrapping all around and through them,
warming their heart and filling them with loving
kindness. Many people find it helpful to visualise
the loving kindness in the form of White Light,
to see this light well up in their own heart and

then to radiate it out like a search light, a beam of light that travels to the other person's heart. Then it fills their heart with the same clear White Light before radiating out and filling their entire body, perhaps even wrapping around them like a cloak or blanket.

If you have difficulty with this, return to the person who loved you most; rekindle, rebuild the feelings of loving kindness you felt from them. Feel it again all through your body and then project that feeling to the neutral person. Keep doing this, moving from one to the other, until you feel the neutral person is as filled with loving kindness as are you and the person who loved you most.

Now imagine a person who has been difficult in your life as if they are before you and on the right of the neutral person. Repeat the exercise, projecting the same feelings of loving kindness to them. If you have difficulty with this, return to the person who loved you the most, re-establish the feelings and then radiate them to the difficult person.

Keep alternating between the three people until the feelings for all three are similiar. You may like to end by resting with the feelings of loving kindness, almost as if you are absorbed in those feelings.

(b) Considering yourself the same as others

The Dalai Lama says this so clearly:

> *"All human beings are the same — made of human flesh, bones and blood. We all want happiness and to avoid suffering. Further, we have an equal right to be happy. In other words, it is important to realize our sameness as human beings."*

Contemplate deeply the fact that in our essence, all human beings are the same. Aim to realise that even the difficult people in our lives are just like us and are seeking the very same things we are. We all wish to be happy. We all wish to be well. Use this deep contemplation to open your heart, to provide insight and generate active compassion.

(c) Walking in the other's shoes

In Buddhism this is called *'Exchanging yourself for others'*. American Indians echo the same sentiment when they say *'Never criticise another before you have walked a mile in their moccasins'*.

This is another key technique I have found helpful for many people. So often we react to the difficult people in our lives with anger and disgust. This exercise has the potential to reframe our view by adding understanding and fostering compassion.

After preparing as if to meditate, imagine
the life of the other person. Where were
they born, what were their parents like?
What type of upbringing might they have
had, what were their formative influences?
What was their childhood like? Their
adolescence? What has been happening for
them recently? What suffering have they
known? How did they get to the point in
life they are at now?

Personally, it has been a very helpful exercise for me to
contemplate in this way the lives of people who perpetrate
crime and bring real suffering into the lives of others. It is
an exercise I found revealing of myself and my previously
ingrained attitudes and prejudices, and one I have felt
great benefit from. I recommend it highly.

(d) Using a friend to generate compassion

This is something of a variation on the previous exercise.

Instead of putting yourself in the other's
shoes, you imagine a dear friend or loved
one in their place. By imagining this
person who is so precious to you, in the
place of someone who is suffering, you
will open your heart and feel moved to be
of direct help.

(e) Considering the suffering of others

It is so easy to be confronted by suffering in this modern world. We travel so much and the media presents so much suffering on a daily basis. Communication is so easy and frequent. Many of us, it seems, deal with this barrage of suffering by attempting to avoid it or by switching off all together. There is a deeply concerning trend that many adults, and especially so many children, are becoming desensitised to suffering. They do not wish to acknowledge it, know it, understand it, or do much about it. It is too much to bear.

How then is it possible to open to the range of suffering around us and to not be overwhelmed? The answers to this crucial question lie in the personal practice of contemplation; in this case the recommendation is to take the time, make the time, to reflect on the nature of suffering itself.

Begin the contemplation on suffering by reflecting upon the fact that everyone suffers in some form or another, just as you do yourself. Notice what reactions you feel and what thoughts come into your mind!

These feelings and thoughts may well challenge you and confront you, but they may also inspire you. Be prepared that being open to this contemplation brings with it vulnerability. It can take you into deep and scary places. It can take you into the mystery of life. It can open profound compassion and this practice may well transform your life.

This practice particularly links into the traditional practice of Tonglen which we will investigate later in this chapter.

(f) How to direct your compassion

The use of the compassion exercises already described is bound to move you towards an even stronger, heartfelt desire to help others. There are two immediate ways to put this heartfelt desire into action.

The first is to fervently pray that all your actions will benefit others and bring them happiness. I felt this prayer was an important part of my healing, I reaffirmed these sentiments every time before I meditated. Now it is the basis of the work I am involved in and I continually remember to come back to it and align my life with its intention in the best way I am able. By prayer in this sense, I mean to repeat your intention over and over. In this sense, it serves as an affirmation and as such will imprint in your mind, guiding your choice of actions to become more and more helpful to others.

The second practice is what Buddhists call Bodhicitta. This means 'to awaken and develop the heart of the enlightened mind' and to dedicate any merit we may have or may develop to the benefit of others.

In this context, what is meant by 'enlightenment', is a mind that is crystal clear, unaffected by past habits, unaffected by ignorance or delusion, unaffected by unhealthy desires or fears. A clear mind. A mind that sees things for what they are, and as a consequence, sees clearly what to do. With such a mind, a 'clear seeing mind' there comes a powerful urge to do all possible to relieve others of suffering and to help them to be truly happy.

With clear seeing comes the knowing true happiness is not about possessions, not about worldly achievements or fleeting pleasures. Sure, these things can be nice but they come and go; they definitely do not guarantee long term happiness. What does guarantee long term happiness is that same crystal clear state of mind. When we contemplate this, we know the truth of it. Happiness is not the result of some "thing"; happiness is a state of mind. We call this state of mind 'enlightenment'.

Therefore we aim to generate our own enlightened state of mind so we can more skilfully, more effectively, more reliably help others to develop their enlightened mind. So while we aim to reach our own enlightenment with the intention of then being more helpful to those around us, we dedicate the merit of that enlightenment towards helping others to reach that same state.

3. Forgiveness

By practising compassion, we become far more aware of the real needs of our self and others. As a consequence, issues of forgiveness commonly arise. In my experience, taking the time to actively generate compassion is often a prerequisite that helps to reveal the importance of forgiveness. Often too, it is the practise of simple meditation and deep compassion that can help to make possible the difficult task of true forgiveness.

Dawn was a very dear friend I had known for many years. When she was diagnosed with bowel cancer, it was already very advanced and there was no effective medical treatment for her. Dawn's condition deteriorated rapidly and I was with her the day she died.

Dawn had lived an extraordinary life. Having been committed to the spiritual path, she had met many great Masters as well as engaging in many personal development practices. As her body had weakened, her spirituality shone forth even more. As she seemed so close to dying, I asked her if she was ready, if there was anything else she needed to do, and how might I help. There was little response to this, so I sensed to ask her if there was anyone she needed to forgive. Dawn reflected for a few moments and said, 'Well yes, there is my father.'

I had known Dawn for many years and it struck me immediately – I had never heard her speak of her father. I asked her what she might need to forgive her father for. She replied, 'Well, he could have been there a bit more for me.'

As we talked on, Dawn elaborated. Her father it seemed, had been a somewhat abusive drunk and her mother had left him when Dawn was only five years old. He had suffered a stroke several years later and died when Dawn was nine. When I asked her how she felt at the time, she said it made little difference for her as, in her mind, he was already dead!

Dawn went on to tell me that in fact her father had remarried and had another daughter before he died. I knew nothing of this half sister's existence and I suspected Dawn's only son did not know her either. To my amazement this actually was the case and I suggested Dawn may like to talk with her son about it all. She agreed and did so later.

What struck me most, however, was how Dawn had done so much personal development and spiritual practice, yet here she was, literally on her deathbed, still holding resentment for her father. I could not help but relate this to the many, many relationships Dawn had entered into with men that lasted a while, but then, more often than not, in fairness, had been fractured by Dawn's own initiative and behaviour.

It seemed easy to link the two. So, here was Dawn, so close to death, her father still unforgiven. I asked her if she could forgive him now. 'Oh yes,' she said, 'that would be easy.' She sighed deeply, lay back, her whole demeanour relaxed and she slept deeply. After she awoke, Dawn spoke with her son and then died peacefully later in the day.

How extraordinary that it was only on her deathbed where forgiveness became possible. And then it was so easy and brought such great relief.

The moral? True forgiveness is difficult. We need to be highly motivated to do it. Once done, however, forgiveness brings a sense of relief and release and a deeply abiding inner peace. Forgiveness has played a key role in the healing of many people who have experienced remarkable recoveries from difficult illness. Also, there is no doubt that forgiveness is a significant key to enduring health and well being.

Why then is forgiveness so hard? To understand this, often we need to begin by understanding what forgiveness is *not*. While in general it is preferable to be positive, there are many misconceptions regarding forgiveness, so to clarify what it is *not,* helps to make forgiveness more possible.

What Forgiveness is not:

i) *Forgiveness is not saying it was OK.* To forgive we need to acknowledge the wrong, the hurt, the injustice. Sometimes we may need to seek reparation in the courts, to bring the offender to justice. We can acknowledge the suffering caused by the act, while forgiving the person.

ii) *Forgiveness is not saying it is OK for it to happen again.* This is a key issue which often I find more of a problem for women than men. The myth is that if you forgive it will happen again. However, forgiveness is clear in saying that it was not OK and that it is not to happen again. Frequently, a challenging part of forgiveness is establishing, or re-establishing personal boundaries. This involves being clear about what you will accept or put up with – and what you will not; and being strong enough in yourself to maintain those boundaries.

iii) *Forgiveness is not forgetting.* While in some situations it can be useful to forget the little hurts and slights and simply move on, we are talking about something different here. When forgiveness involves a major issue, attempts to forget are more likely to take the form of denial. Denial can help short term but it tends to lead to a bottling of emotions with explosions at inopportune times. Forgiveness does not wipe the memory. It does, however, let go of most or all of the pain attending that memory.

iv) *Forgiveness does not mean you have to be friends.* Sometimes forgiveness does clear the air and heals old wounds in a way that allows for the re-establishment of important relationships. This often happens with blood relatives. However, with other people it may well be different.

This reveals a key to the underlying issue which explains why some people find it hard to forgive old partners. While you hang on to resentment, you hang on to the person to whom the resentment is attached. It may not be very pleasant, but you still have the hooks in. You still have an emotional attachment. If you have put a huge emotional investment into this other person and hoped to get something back – if it has not worked out the way you had hoped and you continue to blame them, and hold them in resentment – there is always the outside chance that they may be shamed into realising the error of their ways, to relent, repent or in some other way give something back. Maybe they will even come back.

The challenge with true forgiveness is that it is unconditional. Forgiveness that says 'I will forgive you *if...*' or 'I will forgive you *when...*' is a start, but it is hollow. True forgiveness has no conditions. You have to give it away. It is the same as unconditional love – a gift from the heart. When you feel as if you have been deeply wronged, no wonder forgiveness is so hard!

v) *Forgiveness is not easy.* The point to all this is that to succeed in forgiving, you really have to want to do it. For many I have known it would seem it was not until after they had suffered long and hard at the hands of their own resentment that they were ready to forgive, and in fact realised they needed to forgive.

The Buddhists say being angry with another person is like picking up a hot coal and throwing it at your enemy in the hope of hurting them. At the very least you can be sure the act will hurt yourself, what it does to the other is somewhat in the lap of the Gods! Perhaps we need to suffer the pain of resentment long enough and deep enough before we are clear on the merit of practising forgiveness. Then the work begins.

Preparation for forgiveness

As with most of these key exercises, preparation provides an essential platform or foundation which makes the main practice possible.

For forgiveness, the ideal preparation includes simple meditation, compassion exercises and suffering! Again, for many of us it is only when we see through the ongoing and deep suffering that resentment causes ourselves and others that we become ready to work on forgiveness.

One of the best exercises I find helpful for unsticking some of the resentment glue and allowing an opening to the possibility of forgiveness is the compassion exercise of putting yourself in the other person's shoes. This can help you to understand and feel into what it was that caused the other person to act the way they did, to feel an empathy, a compassion that makes forgiveness more possible. Again, understanding something about the other person's life, their motivations, their actions; understanding the other does not mean you are saying what they did is OK. Far from it. Their actions may have been or continue to be terrible. Acutely terrible. However, you are seeking to understand, to forgive, to lighten your load of resentment, to set new boundaries and to move on.

First and foremost, forgiveness is for your own benefit. It may lead to you becoming a better person; a nicer person to be around; it may lead to you becoming more caring, altruistic, all sorts of good things; but in the first instance, forgiveness will help you directly.

The practice of forgiveness through imagery and affirmation

This exercise was first recorded in *You Can Conquer Cancer*, and is repeated here with some additions. You begin in the standard way, relaxing using the technique of the relaxation response.

Visualise the person you are considering. It can be satisfactory to just concentrate on them, but try to build as clear an image of them in your mind as you can, as if they were sitting in front of you and you were looking directly at them. Some people find it useful to begin by looking at a photograph. This can help to fix the person in your mind.

Then use the following four phrases, repeating each one silently to yourself, over and over, until you can say that phrase with conviction, before going on to the next:

I forgive you.

Please forgive me.

I thank you.

I bless you.

As you begin this exercise, you may notice it takes a little effort to concentrate on the person's image *and* the repetition of 'I forgive you, I forgive you'. However, fairly soon you are likely to settle into the exercise.

Commonly the next step is that you find yourself dwelling on all the good reasons why you should *not* forgive them. 'Forgive *them*! I have every reason to hate that person!' you may think. Every reason, except the hate affects *you* more than anyone else! As you dwell on it more, a wider, healthier perspective will come.

As you keep repeating the phrase, you enter into thinking about why you would benefit from forgiving them. Think of all the reasons why they are like they are, why they did what they did. You will find yourself slipping over into contemplation and a new insight developing. As you continue you *will* reach the point where, with conviction you can say, 'I forgive you!'

Now surprisingly, when I began to practise this exercise, it was the second phase '*Please forgive me*' I found the hardest. While at first I was beset by all the reasons why I should not forgive this person, how horrible they had been, how much they had hurt me and so on; as I persevered I came to realise my own role in all the problems. If I had behaved differently, the whole situation could have developed in a different and maybe more harmonious way. The exercise led to remarkable insights and reframed my whole experience.

Please do be clear here. This is not an invitation for you to feel guilt and shame. To wallow in yet another variation of 'it's all my fault'. What we talk of here is an invitation to a new level of understanding and a generosity of spirit that involves a way of overcoming and transforming one of the most common of human frailties – the tendency to blame others and generate resentment.

In a similar vein, most people find '*I thank you*' to be a major test too. Thanking someone for putting you through a hard time that finally taught you so much demands a perspective of forgiveness and acceptance. This exercise develops a great understanding of life and relationships in general and is why this contemplation exercise takes time. For some, quite a deal of time and quite a deal of perseverance!

'*I bless you*' is easy after the first three have reached the point of conviction. It is a release, a letting go. At this point you recognise the intrinsic worth in the other person. While you may agree to differ on points of view, you are now free to go your independent ways without any negative attachments.

I found it good to start this exercise with easy issues, like the man who cut me off while driving home, the lady who inadvertently stood on my toe or the shop assistant who was so difficult. This is a good thing to do as a regular exercise, choosing one person a day for awhile. I used to recall someone I had met during each day and practise the exercise with them.

Soon I found the whole process with its four phrases echoed in my mind virtually automatically as an incident occurred. If a difficulty with a relationship looked like developing, it was as if those four little phrases whizzed around in my head, defusing the situation even before it developed. Then, as the exercise became well established in this way, I began to work on the harder relationships, the cluttered old ones from times gone by. The effect was considerable. With more time and perseverance I really felt freed of old attachments.

Alcoholics Anonymous takes this idea further in their 12 Step Program and suggests reformed alcoholics need to make restitution with people they have harmed. They recommend actually fronting such people, apologising and doing all they can to physically make good any loss they caused. In my experience it is not essential to go that far unless you choose to. However, I know it works, for there was one particular person who I had been involved with in a difficult way and had not felt comfortable with since. I practised this technique until I really could genuinely say those four statements. When I called on the person, the atmosphere between us was totally different to the usual tension. We fell easily into an extended talk, remarkably doing something we had never done before which was to discuss all our old problems. When we concluded, we both left feeling lighter and happier. It amazed me the whole nature of that relationship was balanced by that exercise.

Many of the people in our groups have found all of this has worked for them and I recommend this exercise in forgiveness highly.

4. Tonglen

This is perhaps the most important of all these exercises due to the potential benefits it offers. This is another exercise that can be difficult to begin as it can reveal many hidden apprehensions, fears and false views you may have been conditioned into holding. Tonglen is not a beginner's practice and a good experience of MBSM is a useful prerequisite. However, it offers a vehicle for major inner work, major inner transformation and the prospect of more fully realising your true nature.

Tonglen is a practise that involves giving and receiving in a way you may not have thought of previously. It is not uncommon for people to recoil from it a little at first, before deeper reflection reveals its merits.

In Tonglen, the aim is to transform the suffering of others into wellbeing and happiness. This is accomplished by taking in all the difficulties of others and giving out your own good qualities. This is done in association with the breath. You breathe in the pain and suffering of others, and breathing out, send them your own inner peace, happiness and wellbeing.

By taking in the suffering of others, especially when that suffering takes the form of emotional pain or physical disease, many people are concerned they might distress themselves, or worse, make themselves sick. What experience demonstrates is this practice does confront these issues, does challenge that ego-based part of our being, does confront our fears. However, here the aim is to break down our ego and to reveal our own good heart. Tonglen very directly does help us to shatter our egos so that we can experience a stronger and more profound level of compassion. This leads you to be able to practise Tonglen even more effectively, with more conviction and impact.

If you choose to practise Tonglen, I highly recommend you study *The Tibetan Book of Living and Dying* so that you can benefit from Sogyal Rinpoche's tradition and experience with this technique. While Tonglen is a

Buddhist practice, it is eminently suitable for everyone.

Sogyal Rinpoche recommends that to begin the practise of Tonglen you do it with yourself first. This is called 'Self Tonglen' and it will help you to learn the technique – to adjust inwardly to the practice – and then you will be more able to practise it with other people. While I have used these practices extensively myself and taught them to others, please acknowledge that I am drawing heavily on Rinpoche's very clear instructions.

Preparing for the practice of Tonglen

Begin in the usual way, as for meditation, and then aim to settle and still your mind as completely as possible. As you allow your thoughts to settle, as you let go and enter into this deeper stillness, you begin to rest in 'the true heart of the enlightened mind.' When you feel ready, begin the practice.

The preliminary exercises of Tonglen

The first of these exercises is intended to clear the atmosphere, the state of mind we are in.

Environmental Tonglen

Be aware of your own state of mind. Notice whatever is moody, dark, angry, frustrated; whatever emotions we normally describe as negative or destructive. Imagine breathing these qualities in on the in-breath, then breathe out the 'positive' or constructive emotions – peace, calm, clarity, joy. Repeat this until you feel the atmosphere around

you, the emotional environment, to be
cleansed.

Next we develop the capacity to transform any destructive emotions within us, releasing in their place love and
compassion.

Self Tonglen

This time, as you breathe in, draw in all
those aspects of your self that you are
unhappy about. Imagine breathing in all
your own hurts, resentments, negativities,
injustices. Now, imagine all that is good
within you receives this suffering. That all
that is good and life-affirming within you
accepts this pain and really feels it all. In
response, your good heart is opened, your
good heart embraces the suffering, absorbs
the suffering. In turn, in response to this,
all the negativity melts away and these
two aspects merge into a mental feeling of
compassion and loving kindness.

Now we can concentrate on liberating our past from
shame and guilt as we develop self-forgiveness.

Tonglen in life

Imagine a situation in life that has left you
feeling shamed or guilty. As you breathe

in, accept responsibility for what you did, without any attempt to rationalise or justify your behaviour. Earnestly ask for forgiveness. Breathe out forgiveness, healing and understanding.

This exercise can reinforce, even add another dimension to the Forgiveness exercise. It is certainly made easier if you have done the latter already, and the two exercises complement each other well.

Finally, the last of the preliminaries involves addressing the pain and suffering others experience.

Tonglen for others

This is like the exercise in Loving Kindness, only this time after you imagine someone who is very close to you, you breathe in their pain and suffering. Breathing out, you send them your own inner peace, love, healing, joy. You then repeat this with the neutral person and the difficult people in your life.

These then were the preliminary practices. By spending time on each one, you will become familiar with the technique and the benefits, and be both inspired and ready to utilise the main practice.

The main practice of Tonglen

1. The preparation. Relax through the relaxation response. Let go of thoughts, allow your mind to settle. Deeply contemplate the nature of compassion, using whichever method works best for you to arouse the strongest feelings of compassion that you can. Invoke the presence of the embodiment of your own truth – whether it be the presence of God, Christ, the Buddha or the more abstract presence of universal love and energy. Feel this all-encompassing presence, all around and through you.

2. Imagine, as if they were in front of you, someone who you care for and who you know is suffering. As you feel your compassion go out to this person, imagine all their problems and difficulties, all their suffering as if it is a cloud of hot, black, grimy smoke or vapour.

3. Now imagine that all your own negativity is like a band or barrier around your own heart. As you breathe in, draw in the black smoke arising from the other person and imagine that it is drawn into that band of negativity around your heart. As it does this it causes all your negativity to dissolve. The band as barrier disintegrates.

4. Imagine that as your negative barrier is dissolved, your own good heart shines forth. This heart is full of radiant, clear white light. As you breathe out, you release this radiant light, car-

rying with it all that is life affirming – peace, joy and happiness. The outbreath carries this light with it to the person you care for and it purifies their negativity on every level. This flow of compassion carries with it the fervent wish to alleviate the suffering of the other person.

By breathing in, you absorb the suffering of the other person; this transforms your own suffering, releasing your finest qualities, which you breathe back to the other. So while your motive is to help the other person, the dual effect is to transform your own inner being.

5. As the light of your heart and compassion touches the other person, feel the deep joy that they have been freed of their pain and suffering. Continue with the practice, breathing in their suffering, breathing out your own healing, love and compassion.

This exercise can be done with anyone. It is an excellent exercise if you want to help someone in need of healing, or someone who may be close to dying. Also, it can transform the way you feel and interact with difficult people in your life. It is a wonderful practice.

Again in Sogyal Rinpoche's words:

> *'This holy secret of the practice of Tonglen is one that the mystic masters and saints of every tradition know; and living it and embodying it, with the abandon and fervour of true wisdom and true compassion, is what fills their lives with joy.'*

CHAPTER 16

IMAGERY AND TRUTH –
What are you really seeking?

RECENTLY, IN A fairly large workshop, I was leading the participants through the series of meditative experiments that so often lead into stillness. These exercises, detailed in *Meditation – Pure & Simple* and *Meditation – an In-depth Guide*, begin by simply observing the thoughts that are present in our own minds. The intention is to notice how your thoughts form – that in fact they form as images made up of pictures, sounds (often words in the form of an inner dialogue) and feelings. Then we notice how each thought is like a segment or unit, with a beginning, a middle and an end point. Next we notice the gap between one thought ending and the next beginning. Of course, in this gap between two thoughts is a moment of silence, so noticing the gap can lead us into this silence, the stillness.

Through direct experience it is possible to realise this stillness has a profoundly spiritual quality. We come to realise this stillness is the sacred ground out of which all things arise and into which all things settle. This is the creative ground of our being. Some will call it God, some will call it the Cloud of Unknowing. Others call it 'the Nature of Mind'; it is the creative ground out of which all things arise and to which all things return when they die.

Having completed the exercises at the workshop, one of the men shared his experience. His eyes were alight, he was sitting forward, almost half standing in the way of someone filled with joyful enthusiasm. His face was radiant as he described what had happened. He had begun to notice his thoughts fairly visually when a new image automatically came to mind. He recalled the toy train of his early childhood. The train had little wooden carriages held together with simple metal links. Now the carriages seemed to represent and carry his thoughts; the links felt as if they were the obvious gaps between the thoughts. As he focussed on the gaps, he focussed on the metal links. These links then proceeded to dissolve. The sense was that as the links dissolved, the carriages followed and soon all that was left was a large fog in front of his eyes.

With a huge smile this man described how he felt he had needed a good deal of courage to enter into this fog. Then, as he spoke on his gaze went inwardly to some distant place, the way people often do when they touch something profound. He said when he was young he had read and remembered a beautiful quote 'All is one, one is all.' He remembered thinking when he first heard it how nice it was; it had touched him deeply, and he had hoped he might come to know it for truth.

With his face beaming, amidst a flurry of awkward giggles and smiles, he said how he had passed through the fog to a state where that oneness was revealed to him by direct experience. Having said this, he could say no more. He was mildly overwhelmed, mildly ecstatic. Deeply joyful. Radiant.

So as we come to the end of this work – a summary, some encouragement and some final suggestions.

Imagery is to do with the mind. Imagery is the language of the mind. Imagery is the tool of the mind. The mind is extraordinarily powerful. What we have come to learn through our investigation of the mind and the manner in which it works is that the mind is a double-edged sword – it can be powerfully destructive, powerfully creative.

For many of us, the conditioning of past experiences, the conditioning stored in our memory as images, limits the capacity of our mind. For many of us, to actively work on training our mind and reprogramming our mind is therefore a key step in freeing us from past limitations and opening us to future possibilities. Clearly, it is the mind that changes everything.

However, if we limit ourselves to what the thinking mind alone is capable of, we limit ourselves to what can be rationalised, analysed, broken into smaller pieces or built up with methodical planning. While this may well have its benefits, clearly it has its limitations. For the truth of the matter is that the essence of life, the heart of life, is essentially mysterious.

Love, hope, faith, all that we really value, all that has true substance and meaning; all these qualities have about them the air of mystery and they dwell in that other aspect of the mind. They dwell in the realm beyond the thinking mind.

Once again then, we return to the need for balance. Yes, it makes sense, profound sense, to rationally address the workings of the thinking mind as we have done in this book. And yes, it makes sense to understand the key role of images and imagery in our lives and to use this understanding with more awareness, with more good effect. It makes sense to train our minds. And clearly too, for completeness and for the opportunity of finding what we are really looking for, we need to go beyond the thinking mind, perhaps using imagery as the vehicle to transport us into the magical essence of our own true self! The essential nature of our mind. Bon Voyage!

RESOURCES

When it comes to practising the many exercises in this book, you will find some are easy to do having read the directions. Others are more complex and it can be helpful to listen to them so that you are guided and supported to focus on the inner work. You may therefore find it helpful to use the text as a basis for making your own recordings. I have recorded the key imagery exercises and there are also a number of CDs available to help you with your meditation practice.

Details are available at www.iangawler.com.au

INDEX OF 48 TECHNIQUES
AND EXERCISES

ACKNOWLEDGEMENTS

I WOULD LIKE to thank David Khan who has done a great job with the cover. Also many thanks to Pam Cossins who is an exceptional typesetter and a wonderful help in all aspects of the writing. My wife Ruth is a constant source of love and inspiration. She has a well trained, critical eye when it comes to do with things of the mind. Her input, her positive feedback and her proof reading have been invaluable. Thanks too to my publisher Mark Zocchi who has been a delight to work with and has done a wonderful job putting it all together. Paul Bugeja as editor made a valuable contribution in clarifying and ordering the manuscript.

A final, heartfelt thanks for all those who have shared their stories in this book. I have changed everyone's names except for Debbie Flintoff-King. Debbie's story is very much in the public domain and I thank her for sharing it again in this forum.

I trust that any merit that flows from this book flows to those wonderful people who I have taught and who have taught me.

Ian Gawler
February 2011

BIBLIOGRAPHY

Clynes, M., *Sentics – The Touch of Emotions*, Garden City, New York, Anchor Press Doubleday, 1978.

Doidge, N., *The Brain That Changes Itself*, Carlton North, Scribe, 2008.

Dossey, L., *Healing Words*, San Francisco, Harper Collins 1993.

Frankl, V., *Man's Search for Meaning*, New York, Pocket Books, 1963.

Gawler, Ian, *You Can Conquer Cancer*, Melbourne, Hill of Content, 1984. Revised edition: Melbourne, Michelle Anderson Publishing, 2001.

Gawler, Ian, *Peace of Mind*, Melbourne, Hill of Content, 1987. Revised edition: Melbourne, Michelle Anderson Publishing, 2002.

Gawler, Ian, *Meditation – Pure & Simple*, Melbourne, Hill of Content, 1996.

Gawler, Ian & Bedson, Paul, *Meditation – an In-depth Guide*, Melbourne, Allen & Unwin, 2008.

Krystal, P., *Cutting the Ties That Bind*, Maine, Samuel Weiser, Inc. 1993.

Maltz, M., *Psycho-Cybernetics*, Sydney, Bantam, 1978.

Meares, A., *Relief Without Drug: The Self-Management of Tension, Anxiety and Pain*, London, Collins/Fontana, 1967.

Meares, A., *The Wealth Within*, Melbourne, Hill of Content, 1978.

Pert, C., *Molecules of Emotion*, New York, Touchstone, 1997.

Siegel, D., *The Mindful Brain*, New York, Norton, 2007.

Simonton, O.C., Matthews-Simonton, S. & Creighton, J.L., *Getting Well Again*, Sydney, Bantam, 1978.

Sogyal Rinpoche, *The Tibetian Book of Living & Dying*, London, Rider, 1992.

Yongey Mingyur Rinpoche & Swanson E., *The Joy of Living*, New York, Harmony Books/Random House, 2007.

The Australian Concise Oxford Dictionary, Melbourne, Oxford University Press, 1987.

The Holy Bible, Revised Standard Edition, New York, Thomas Nelson, 1972.

ABOUT THE AUTHOR

Dr Ian Gawler OAM
BVSc, MCounsHS

IAN GAWLER HAS played a major part in popularising meditation, Mind–Body Medicine and other self-help techniques in the western world. Ian is one of Australia's best known, long term cancer survivors and advocates of a healthy lifestyle. His story offers hope and inspiration to people around the world. The self-help techniques he developed have helped many to convert hope into sustained health and peace of mind. A pioneer in Mind–Body Medicine and the therapeutic application of meditation, Dr Gawler has written widely on these subjects and presented his work to many major conferences. With a gift for translating ancient wisdom into a modern context, and having appeared widely in the media, Ian is known for his clarity and good humour.

Ian Gawler has studied meditation with Dr Ainslie Meares, His Holiness the Dalai Lama and Sogyal

Rinpoche as well as a wide range of leading Buddhist, Indian, Zen, Christian and other Western Meditation Masters. He is a long-term student of his main teacher, Sogyal Rinpoche, the author of *The Tibetan Book of Living and Dying*. Ian's teachings combine the intellect of the West with the insight of the East.

As well as a degree in Veterinary Science, Ian holds a Masters in Counselling and Human Services.

In 1987 Ian Gawler was awarded the Order of Australia Medal for his services to the community.

QTY

The Mind that Changes Everything $26.99 ……..

Postage within Australia (1 book) $5.00………
Postage within Australia (2 or more books) $9.00………

TOTAL* $_____

* All prices include GST

Name: ....

Address: ....

Phone: ....

Email Address: ....

Payment:

❏ Money Order ❏ Cheque ❏ Amex ❏ MasterCard ❏ Visa

Cardholder's Name:..

Credit Card Number: ....

Signature:..

Expiry Date: ....

Allow 21 days for delivery.

Payment to: Better Bookshop (ABN 14 067 257 390)
          PO Box 12544
          A'Beckett Street, Melbourne, 8006
          Victoria, Australia
          betterbookshop@brolgapublishing.com.au

BE PUBLISHED

Publishing through a successful Australian publisher. Brolga provides:
- Editorial appraisal
- Cover design
- Typesetting
- Printing
- Author promotion
- National book trade distribution, including sales, marketing and distribution through Macmillan Australia.

For details and inquiries, contact:
Brolga Publishing Pty Ltd
PO Box 12544
A'Beckett St VIC 8006

Phone: 03 9600 4982
bepublished@brolgapublishing.com.au
markzocchi@brolgapublishing.com.au
ABN: 46 063 962 443